SALESMAN ON FIRE

By

Carson V. Heady

Cover art by Jo Otey

Acknowledgements

For my family – You are the reason I give my all.

For sellers and leaders everywhere – I've been so blessed to make so many connections in this community. You inspire me more than you'll ever know. Thank you for everything you have taught me.

We are so fortunate to be students of the selling game.

Contents

Re-commitment.

It's powerful and crucial. Sometimes it is needed daily… or weekly, or monthly. Sometimes we have to slow it down so much that it's re-committing moment to moment.

It could be re-commitment to our faith, to spouse or significant other, to family, to friends or to purpose.

It could be to our career or job, or re-committing in light of changes.

It can be re-adjusting our sails amidst rough waters or re-evaluating after substantial shifting of our circumstances – fair or unfair.

It can be re-committing to process or regimen or lifestyle choices or religion or diet.

Re-commitment reaffirms our priorities despite what's past or where we made a misstep.

It can be done in spite of our initial feelings on the matter.

It's done because it's what we choose to do, what we have to do, or what we want to do.

Re-commitment signals that in this moment, we are committing to a course of action. We are throwing our energy into seeing this commitment through with a leap of faith the momentum will carry us forward.

Re-committing requires strength and courage.

Re-committing is sometimes all we have.

FOREWARD

The *Birth of a Salesman* series has been a tremendous blessing over the past decade. As a direct result of these books, I have had distinct career path and relationship ramifications that have enriched my life.

Salesman on Fire is a reflection on a body of work; a sum of the parts.

I started writing *Salesman on Fire* in 2019, prior to the 2020 Coronavirus pandemic and its subsequent effect globally on people, communities, health professionals, every form of business and nearly everything in our world.

Some were infected but all were affected.

Many brave folks fought the virus on the front lines, leaders made difficult decisions and organizations everywhere scrambled to keep goods and services flowing and available. No industry or company or person was left untouched or unchanged.

Businesses had to react, respond and evolve and many were hampered or crippled in the wake of shutdowns. Thousands died in many countries and millions lost their jobs.

Sales took on a whole new meaning.

Entire organizations shifted to remote work where they could, amidst all the security and compliance questions that shift would beget.

Many sellers and customers – and people in all levels of organizations – were working remotely, from home, on stay-at-home orders home-schooling children and caring for others all while unable to or advised not to see other loved ones.

Parks were closed. Sports came to a halt.

And the role of a seller – and that of a leader – changed dramatically overnight.

Sales became *only* about relationships. Checking up on clients and contacts, trying to add value in any way possible. Many were laid off amidst uncertain economic times.

Leaders saw a storm the likes of which they had never seen – perhaps leading remote resources for the first time, certainly managing employees with varying levels of concern and fear, and they were charged with trudging forward with their teams into uncertain territory.

If one common learning can emerge for all of us, it's the power of relationships and connection. Relationships were strengthened despite not being together in person. For many, the memory of handshake or a face-to-face meeting made them long for things to go 'back to normal.'

But like a long and winding career or life, there is no going back and there is no return to "normal" – there's only a new path forward. Inevitably, the world will not be the same. We can control how we infuse the learnings and positive takeaways into the future versions of ourselves and what we can influence.

Many industries and companies have been forced to alter the way they engage their customers and it will forever change their business.

Different isn't always better, but better is always different. Some of the changes that have transpired will stick and will provide a better, more advanced or even just a virtual path that did not exist before.

No matter what, everyone who was affected amidst these trying times, will emerge with a new perspective that will inform future interactions.

And we'll certainly all have a fresh appreciation for the things we missed.

"We rejoice in our sufferings, knowing that suffering produces endurance, and endurance produces character, and character produces hope." - Romans 5: 3-4

Chapter 1: A Meeting in Minneapolis

Sometimes all you have to do is ask.

I'm a firm believer in the ability to connect with just about anyone thanks to the tools we have access to in this digital age.

I have known of *the* Vincent Scott for some time. We ran in different circles in different cities but occasionally in the same industry over the last couple of decades. Thanks to a LinkedIn request one of us sent (I don't think either of us remembers who), we connected years ago.

Specifically, as he wrote *The Selling Game* and became a prolific speaker and influencer, I followed his career with great interest. And, then, of course, I was able to get enough access to him to craft *Birth of a Salesman* 10 years ago. That changed my life, and I know it changed his. Inadvertently, I became Watson to his Holmes.

Our lives and careers certainly went on dizzying paths in the decade since, but we kept in touch from time to time; typically a note nearing the holidays or a touch base to wish the other well – when there were births in our families or changes in career. We engaged with each other's social media posts that were personal and professional in origin. We kept abreast of one another as best we could.

One of my 2020 resolutions was to take a jump into a foray of better and more impactful connections, specifically with those I have identified as mentors over the years. Vincent Scott was at the top of my list.

I requested to get together with him, either virtually or in person and not knowing what to expect. Aware of Vincent's moves over the years, including with some major companies, and not 100% sure what he was currently focused on, I figured at the very least, I could see how the years had impacted his journey and philosophies.

He writes, he blogs, and I knew he had been promoted a couple of times in recent years, but it would be good to catch up – especially given our history. We were due for our 10-year reunion.

Vincent was responsive (he typically is, not that I have any idea how considering the demands on his time between family, career and side hustle) and it turned out I would be in Minneapolis on business during a time that was conducive for him to get together. He offered me a day in the life to just hang out, as I was preparing to launch whatever this project turns out to be. I gratefully accepted.

There were no visions at the time that this would transform into more or less a biography of Vincent Scott, the greatest salesperson I've ever known.

My Minneapolis trip was business-related, but I always have vacation time to burn or lose so I had no qualms about scheduling a day off so I could tag along with Vincent Scott – whatever that would look like. It would be great to see what was new in his world, but it was also the first time I would see him in person in 10 years.

Knowing Vincent, I am aware he is pragmatic and married to routine and I was taking him out of it for a day. My primary desire was to inconvenience him as little as possible.

We agreed to meet for breakfast at the Hell's Kitchen on South 9th Street at 9 AM – leaving plenty of time for morning workouts and commutes. He indicated little of his agenda for the day outside of a couple of stops he needed to make, dinner at his house and that he'd be able to take me to the airport in the evening. He would be able to get me there in time to allow him to get back and stay with their youngest daughter so his wife could take their oldest to volleyball.

Ironically, just that piece alone was indicative of the shift in Vincent's tectonic plates over the past decade. When I got to know him initially, Vincent was an early-30's bachelor with a young daughter and a penchant for late hours and his fair share of nightlife. This Vincent was nearing 42 years old, a far cry from the 20's sales phenom who came out of nowhere to earn promotion after promotion, write books and give speeches.

Vincent Scott was a middle-aged journeyman sales leader. He had taken his talents to companies big and small. He wrote books, authored columns, penned blogs and clearly had been through a considerable number of ups and downs personally and professionally. He was now married with two kids, once again leading a sales team at a large organization. The rest was for me to discover.

Vincent was the one who brought my attention to the Orson Welles quote, "If you want a happy ending, that depends, of course, on where you stop your story."

"Are you sure you want to upset our last ending?" he mused, jokingly, in our most recent phone call.

For Vincent had risen the ranks quite quickly – 3 promotions in his first 6 years – at ABM Worldwide. The youngest director in the company's history, Vincent was infamous amongst sellers who worshiped him and notorious with senior leadership who misunderstood him. He was a crusader for his people amidst shady practices of bureaucratic buffoons. He took countless sales teams to unbelievable heights amidst countless roadblocks.

Vincent was writing a weekly column for ABM's advertising bureau newsletter and had a strong hand in forming a brand-new division to sell advertising solutions in the offseason of their field marketing teams. He was on top of the world until he very abruptly wasn't.

Vincent stood up to a crooked department head and – despite being on the right side of things – was fired.

We first met in the year he spent between ABM and the Brink Management organization he aligned with in 2011. After a tumultuous year there featuring a very swift rise followed by a gradual epic fall, he had big wins with two subsequent organizations including Tel-Cell Wireless and Majestech-Ware Global. He had continued to add countless awards and accolades, has been interviewed on every sales and leadership podcast I can think of and yet he never indicated to me that he felt like he had fully gotten over the disappointment after ABM.

The concept of figuring out where he found himself now was certainly intriguing to me. I had no doubt it would be interesting and entertaining; I always appreciated his perspective on sales and leadership, but also his constant thirst for more. He was certainly a Type A personality who thrived when he was on a unique, specific mission but always looked for fresh challenges. There was no one like him.

When my cab dropped me off and I arrived at Hell's Kitchen, I could see Vincent was already there. He was in a suit – bluish-grey – with a multi-colored patterned shirt, no tie. Vincent looked up from his phone. He smiled.

Placing the phone in his jacket pocket, Vincent rose to greet me.

Vincent Scott still retained most of the boyish charm in his face and features but looked more worn and tired. He still had nearly all of his blondish hair – it slightly thinned in places. There was a bit of greying at the temples. He was looking fit.

His face lit up with a half smirk that turned into a full-blown smile.

"Carson," he said. "It's been a long time."

"It has," I replied, taking his outstretched hand. I noticed that Vincent often took the approach of extending his hand in a way that forced yours to be on top of his. He intentionally, psychologically ceded the importance of the interaction to the recipient of his handshake. This time was no different. "Thank you for making time to meet with me."

"Of course," Vincent said, gesturing back toward the table. We took a seat. There were waters already at the table. "I trust your trip in was OK?"

"It was. Uneventful," I replied, taking a sip of water and glancing at the menu. "I got in yesterday. Had a meeting in the afternoon, stayed at the Millennium, had room service. Up this morning and hit the gym. What's good here?"

"Everything, but as I, too, was able to get my workout in this morning I am opting for the Crawfish Eggs Benedict and a biscuit with gravy." He grinned, clearly relishing the thought of indulging during his favorite meal of the day.

"That sounds exquisite."

We situated ourselves and exchanged some additional pleasantries.

"So, tell me more about what you're working on here," Vincent requested, motioning toward my phone set to record and laptop ready for notes.

"Sure! Honestly, I don't know what to expect from it. I'm trying to keep a 2020 resolution to dive more fully into personal growth. Learning from mentors. That sort of thing. As a part of that, I just want to spend time with mentors either virtually or in person and glean enough to do an article or a book or whatever this turns into."

"I'm honored you considered me," Vincent said.

"Well, absolutely," I offered. "Would certainly not have embarked on anything like this without talking to you. That said, just hearing how Vincent Scott views the world these days and finding out what you're up to is fascinating enough for me."

"You've caught me at an interesting time," Vincent said, almost hesitant but nevertheless committed to the words.

"Don't I usually?" I asked, half-jokingly but not said in a way to insult him in any way. "That is a good portion of my amazement with you, Vincent. No matter what you do, your journey unravels in fascinating and wondrous ways. Much deserved, I might add."

"I pray that continues," he replied, continuing the near trepidation as the waiter came to collect our orders.

We continued with a few moments of catching up on each other's lives, kids, hobbies. To hear Vincent Scott relay the rigors of raising a pre-teen and 3-year old girl with his wife, to talk about church, to talk about exercise regimen and the near-constant activity devoted to faith, family and working was quite the stark contrast of the stories of his 20's. He had transformed considerably in the last decade, but even a great deal just over the last few years.

"So how do you want to do this?" Vincent asked.

"I figured I'd ask a few questions, and with very little forced framework let you talk about whatever you deem most prudent," I proffered.

"That works for me. You know when I do and don't prefer structure," he laughed.

"So... Vincent Scott," I shifted my tone to sound a bit more official, "You've spent a career in sales and leadership. First – how did it begin?"

Between bites of breakfast and sips of juice, Vincent relayed a familiar story – most of which I could have recited but I dared not interrupt.

Vincent had set out to work in a customer service role fresh off moving from Mankato, MN, to Minneapolis in the waning weeks of summer 2001. His lifelong friend's aunt was a director at ABM and introduced him to a recruiter. Vincent met with her, made his case for employment and outlined his goals and was fast-tracked for a role in a call center.

What he thought would be customer service-oriented wound up being extremely high pressure sales in a call center fielding calls from business owners (and very soon residential customers) often complaining about their bills and being expected to sell them phone and Internet packages. He was in a training class of 12 where only 2 made it out.

"If anything, that was my first real taste of how important perseverance is to the sales game," Vincent mused. "It was survival of the fittest and frankly most people who have any way out of something hard will take it.

"I had to pay my dues. I distinctly remember talking to my parents and even to the director who recommended me for the job about how I didn't think I could do it. I wanted to quit.

"At 22, I had – up to that point – lived a pretty coddled existence. I had been fortunate to do well in school quite easily and spent six years at a grocery store in Mankato moving through different departments. This was my first real taste of Corporate America and I wasn't necessarily prepared for that level of intensity.

"But, like many things, if you can weather the storm you're around for the spring. I noticed the energy in that dead call center change. There was competition. There was a new vibe – an excitement. Noise. Amazingly, as hard as it was for me to acclimate to the place and the pace, I effortlessly became the top rep in the office.

"People that had been there for years and years were now awakened. Their previous top reps were gunning for me, making excuses as to why they couldn't beat me. Now I was the one with the target on my back.

"All I had was a gift for gab; I didn't care about the technology or the concepts or the outcomes. I felt like I cared about the customer's satisfaction, but it was a means to an end. What really happened was I got my first taste of any real money and how in control of my own paycheck and destiny I felt. It was euphoric – at times. Until we had to work seven days a week."

Vincent spent 6 quarters as a phone sales rep, winning an award for being in the top 5% in the company every quarter. Managers in the division changed. The new director took a liking to him and promoted him to management in early 2003.

"It began by accident," Vincent summarized. "It was unlike anything I had encountered and was not what I expected. But it certainly led me in a direction that unfolded into everything I have now and everything I've been blessed to be able to do."

"Anything you'd do differently about those early days and years?" I inquired.

"My gosh," Vincent laughed. "That's a catch-22. Anything done differently would change the learning or experiences. I sometimes wish I had not been as naïve or brash. Perhaps I got a false sense of reality by moving up so quickly. I also wish I had made more strategic, meaningful relationships. I was too trusting and talked too much. I had no idea how to play the game and to build the type of network that I'd need later.

"It took me a long time to understand how important playing the political game was and is."

"How so?"

"Whatever we think of our jobs, we're accepting a paycheck for a role we agreed upon. We have a contract with our employer to do that role and to be ambassadors of our company. We may disagree with what comes down and if we're lucky, we get a chance to voice our concerns and opinions. But when a ruling is final, it's final, and we have to execute. Period.

"Some companies do better jobs than others of soliciting us for our feedback. But at the end of the day, we're paid for that job and if we step too far out of bounds, we become expendable. I really wish I had known then how to better 'play the game'; how to better conduct myself with poise and polish. How to not take so many cavalier liberties just because I was good at getting results and leading people. There was a whole other element I was missing – being a steward of my organization whether I liked it or not, whether I agreed with it or not."

"Give me an example."

"I've had managers throughout my career that I didn't see eye to eye with, for whatever reason. Each experience was painful, but I made it more painful in those early days because I rebelled. I talked back. I thought I was so special I could say or do whatever I wanted because they needed me so badly. I was gravely mistaken.

"While I was valuable, I put myself at risk from time to time and sullied my own reputation with recklessness. Eventually, I had the screws put to me and was taken out, but I could have done it differently. Sure, that final situation was in the face of illegal activity by my boss, but I still could have handled it all better. I thought I was invincible and would get his job when they got rid of him. That didn't happen.

"Again, though, how could I change any of it? My pastor spoke not long ago about being as thankful for our curses as for our blessings. My carelessness and trusting the wrong people and my missteps made me too vulnerable. But it all led me to where I am; without the rough spots there would have been no books and no path to the jobs and adventures I've had since.

"That said, I also certainly cannot believe I had the audacity to write a book about sales in my twenties."

We snickered about that one for a moment.

"Why were you promoted – not only at first, but continuously through your career?" I asked.

"The division I was in had been through a lot of change and endured a lot," Vincent said after a moment's consideration. "In fact, we had to shut down and go back through training just to switch from business to residential focus.

"I'm a process guy. I believed I could get something out of every single call. On the one hand, I embraced a strategy of offering something on every call but where the company wanted to force a generic offer I had an uncanny ability of scanning the account, figuring out what I could get from a probability perspective, and converting sales more often than anyone else. Far more.

"Facets of what I was doing were contagious as well. I benefited from a changing of the guard in the office; some old hands quit or were fired. I was what management wanted because I was proof that the job could be done and the numbers could be crushed, which was contradictory to the excuses the old team was giving. I could be held up as an example of what was possible.

"I did it my way – it was not exactly in line with how the company wanted it done from a call flow perspective. Fortunately, the planets aligned, I got a manager who let me do whatever I needed to do and a new director who thought I could help others replicate my results. I was young but so was my director – relatively – and she took a chance on me. It paid off. For both of us.

"As for subsequent promotions, I attribute a fair amount of luck, connecting and personal branding. It was never enough for me to do a job – if my name was next to numbers on a report, they had to be indicative of my best. Pride in my work is a supremely driving force.

"Something that shocks most people is in my life, I've applied to well over 2,000 jobs. I was a manager for a couple of years and was itching to do something else; I get very restless if things aren't moving. I'm not always proud of it. But I continuously have to be doing something where I feel like I'm adding unique value, influencing as many people as I can and being noticed and rewarded. That mix is tough to come by. And sometimes you run out of challenges in the job you're in.

"I applied internally to probably 100+ jobs in 2005. I was salty because a peer I beat every month on the sales report who was most known for his sneaky termination methods against anyone not crushing goal got promoted over me – because he played the game better. He sidled up to our boss effectively, said all the right stuff and made no waves with management. Our boss was incompetent, so I did a poor job of getting in her good graces. The division seemed to reward those who disciplined and terminated based on their flawed call flow, and I wouldn't do it. So, I wanted to transfer out, but no one was giving me the time of day.

"Getting a promotion is an art, just like getting a job. The system is set up to eliminate candidates and warm referrals are preferred because they are vouched for by trusted sources.

"Knowing that your probability of getting any job is low and that the burden of proof is on you to show why you're uniquely qualified is just part of the battle. The other part is how well you can politically position yourself for the hiring manager – be it an endorsement by someone they trust or by making the evidence in your favor so overwhelming they have to hire you.

"Either way, you have to understand that no matter how good of a match you think you are for something, nothing is *ever* a slam dunk. I've been promised promotions that never came. I was told a role was created specifically for me and then it was given to someone else. I was recruited for multiple jobs and told the offer was coming only to never get it. For every win I've had, I've had a hundred disappointments – if not a thousand. Sales and leadership, like life and love, are heartbreaking. But enough good comes out of the relationships and the learnings that it keeps you coming back.

"My second promotion at ABM was actually an internal role I applied for. I don't necessarily believe in luck per se, but more that we can create our own luck in perseverance and the brand we put out there.

"Fortunately, I was always tweaking my résumé and applying to roles and messaging hiring managers asking for a conversation. Over time, I've bettered – I would not say perfected – that craft; meaning, I know to ask for advice or an informational or feedback or guidance as opposed to making my case in an e-mail for why I want or should get the job. *Get in the room before you do the selling.* Try to get in as many rooms as possible."

When Vincent spoke, specifically on items he felt particularly passionate about, his hand gestures would increase in frequency and speed.

"I thought my résumé was irresistible and my skills and accomplishments could get me in any door – both when I was at ABM and after. I was dead wrong," he continued, sitting back in his chair in reflection. "Luckily, ABM Advertising started a new department designed to cold call every business they could get their hands on in the offseason of the field marketing reps and they needed a few good sales managers. Their new GM met with me, liked what I had to say, and I eventually came on board in March 2006. That promotion changed my life.

"That's where I met, interviewed and hired my wife Abby. That's where I came to realize how much I personally could influence and move the needle in tens of millions of dollars. That's where I gained what I thought was power. I just had no idea how to use it. And I let it get to my head.

"My promotions since have been because I was far and away the best from a results perspective and – in recent years – because I became relatively disciplined. Though as I alluded to, I've had my fair share of continued setbacks. When you're at the top, you're a target, and not everyone wants to promote someone who is a better leader than they are. Secure leaders want a succession plan and they want to build their dream team, but insecure managers want puppets or followers. They pay the price in results.

"My promotions were a result of understanding the playing field very well and how to best manage my results based on the parameters. There's a fair amount of hustle stats and keeping a consistent hand on the wheel no matter the roadblocks. And there was endurance – staying in a role I had mastered sometimes long after I had mastered it and earned consideration for a promotion.

"Nothing worth anything ever happens on our timetable. It happens when it's supposed to happen if at all. And if it's not this role you think you want, it is something else down the road that may have yet to show itself. If you work hard and you put yourself in the right conversations, you'll create opportunities. I've been blessed to create a lot."

"That's the second time you said 'blessed' and you mentioned involvement in church earlier. That's not something I recall you talking about in our previous dialogue. If you're comfortable sharing, what does that mean to you?" I asked.

"I was raised Catholic," Vincent answered quickly. "I've always believed in God and talked to God, but I did it on my terms when I felt like it. My parents enrolled me in Catholic school and Catholic high school growing up, so I was in church 3 times a week. Its importance was a bit lost on me because I didn't relate to the older priests. The messages didn't resonate. While I did once do a youth group pilgrimage to see the Pope, I didn't at all understand my relationship with God at this level until the last couple of years.

"My wife and I had different religious backgrounds, making finding a church in Minneapolis we agreed upon somewhat challenging. As it turned out, our oldest daughter Elizabeth tried out for a play at our current church – a Lutheran one – and we attended service there months later because the people there had struck us as quite pleasant. They were very welcoming; we had our kids baptized there and then we became members. It's been one of the best things to ever happen for me and for our family at a time I think I really needed that type of peace and comfort."

"Why is that?" I inquired. This part of the story was very new to me.

"When did we last chat in depth – 2016?"

I nodded. "Your team had just landed a massive deal and you were recruited to run a new division under Majestech-Ware's then-CEO Miranda Bond."

Vincent chuckled. "Yeah, so you saw where some of that panned out..." he trailed off.

Miranda Bond was with the company just 3 months longer until they were purchased by CTMI.

"I've been 'on top of the world' just a few times in my life, and it never lasts long," Vincent mused, reflectively. "Which is why I've learned to just focus on the day, the journey."

Vincent paused again to take a bite of egg and sip his coffee. I said nothing.

"The nice thing about Majestech-Ware was that deal, coupled with my team's performance as tops in the world for 8 quarters in a row provided some financial security. But no job is secure. Heck, I thought I'd be at ABM forever.

"But I can tell you that if the last 10 years have given me anything it's fewer friends but closer and real ones. A *real* network and brand. Perspective. It's knowing how to keep focus on winning the moment and mastering the day as opposed to obsessing over what I want to achieve 6 months from now. I've lost friends and jobs and belief in a lot of the things I worshipped in my 20's but faith and hope in a grander purpose keeps the most tragic or unexpected events in their proper place."

"I want to know where that part of the story goes," I said, "but I think it's important to table set first. What makes you tick?"

"Faith, family, friends, and making a difference. Making an impact. Influencing. Imparting what I've learned so that someone else can succeed. And having experiences. As many new ones as I can."

"I'd say that needle has shifted a bit as well?"

"Absolutely."

"Are you close with your extended family?"

"More than ever. We've lost some family members over the last couple of years, but I think it makes us cherish each other more. I have never been closer with my own parents, but that has come with age and becoming a parent myself. I understand their plight so much better now and regret how I acted as a teenager and in my 20's. I love my in-laws, too. I take as much time with family as I can.

"Experiences are critical, too. I chased money and what I thought was power so much in my 20's that I got lost in work. I made it my identity, which is why it so easily came crashing down when I had it taken from me. I became reckless with it. I thought people were my friends that weren't. I crossed the wrong people. They crushed me.

"I actually had a profound and needed epiphany during a great experience – an adventure – just a couple of years back..." Vincent's mind was clearly taking him back.

"Tell me about that!"

"All in the proper context," he said. "I should really start where we left off."

In early 2016, after Vincent's team closed a $57M hardware deal, Vincent was recruited to a Sales Optimization VP role by the CEO of Majestech-Ware.

The ink was barely dry on the deal when talks of an acquisition by Corporate Technology Marketing, Inc. started. Vincent had hardly gotten his bearings in the new role: understanding the ecosystem, how Majestech-Ware business solutions worked across the enterprise, the players and the programs. He met his team, started to learn the reports and started teaching folks how to better prospect and create processes for metric improvement. And then CTMI bought out Majestech-Ware and Miranda Bond retired.

In merger and acquisition situations, it is often commonplace that redundant roles and layers of management are eliminated; companies like Majestech-Ware with a global presence tend to cost a pretty penny. CTMI possessed a COO and CMO and VP of Sales and felt they would not need to acquire Vincent's price tag and VP of Sales Optimization role when this could just roll up through sales.

Furthermore, despite the need for an Area Director and Vincent's dozen years at various levels of sales leadership, Vincent was reclassified as a Territory Manager for the bulk of the southern half of Minnesota (including Minneapolis, St. Paul and even hometown Mankato). The VP of Sales for CTMI, Floyd Irving, brought in a friend and confidante from the marketing team in Mexico to fill the Area Director role, managing Vincent and his dozen peers. Her name was Quintana Navarro. It was her first management role at age 42. She would report to GM John Deever.

While Vincent was glad to still have a role and had certainly been through mergers and acquisitions before while with ABM and Cellular Horizons, he had paid tremendous dues in his last Regional Business Manager role to earn the VP tag he carried. It had been an appointment directly from a well-respected CEO, so to see it dissipate so quickly and so easily was a tough pill to swallow.

It was August 2016 and Vincent had already learned that his wife Abby was pregnant with their second child due March 2017. He needed job stability right now and was open that he could learn from the viewpoint of Quintana. She had worked with some of the CTMI vendors Vincent would now collaborate with and she spent a lot of time with Vincent's new VP of Sales, so he'd focus and play the game the way he had learned to do. Open-minded, slow to speak and quick to collaborate.

Vincent's role was now to manage the account teams covering 200+ small-to-midsize accounts in the southern half of Minnesota. There were numerous industry verticals represented and his specialist team would consist of account managers, sellers on specific CTMI products (they sold everything from hardware to productivity tools and niche offerings around artificial intelligence and data) and he managed all vendor activity in that patch. Deals went through him, incentives went through him, and he would often manage relationships with C-Suite within his territory.

"I made a mistake in the early going," Vincent admitted. He paused to take another substantial bite of food, collect his thoughts and consume beverages. "I did too much. I think I felt like I had to tackle this thing better than anyone else could. My predecessors in this territory hadn't hit goal in 5 years. I set up as many meetings with C-Suite, leaders in the business and folks in IT as I possibly could as quickly as I could. I met with a third of these 230 accounts personally within the first couple of months – it was unheard of. I was also trying to sign new accounts, trusting that the account teams and vendors were doing their job upselling into the accounts – and they weren't. I was working 60-80 hours a week during my first year of marriage with a kid on the way, sometimes triple- and quadruple-booked and always back-to-back all day every day.

"Nobody trained me. And Quintana had never done the job, so she was really only focused on forecast and pipeline. That's all she knew, and it's all unpopular and brash Floyd Irving ever asked about. Ironically, I was on a pipeline review call with Floyd my first week on the job and – as I knew very little about the territory yet – he belittled and insulted me, oblivious to the fact I had just begun. A real people person.

"Quintana would urge us to commit more deals to close during certain times of the quarter and fiscal year to make her forecast look better. She'd also question why deals in the territory were committed to close when there was not an exact date for signature – she'd say they had to have timeline, budget and power. She'd hammer me on what I was doing to drive more pipeline. I'd tell her the numerous activities I was engaging in, and she said 'no, the vendor engine needs to be doing everything *for* you.' They obviously weren't despite my best efforts.

"She was quite confusing. She made more and more evident that she had no idea what she was talking about.

"Quintana would speak to vendors and it was evident they were just as confused by her diatribe. She'd go off on some tangent about what she viewed our company story was, as if these vendors hadn't built their entire business off of what we do. And she clearly did not understand how to truly utilize a vendor relationship in these accounts. They would give me weird looks during any meeting we were in together when she was preaching to them. It was very uncomfortable. But I had to humor it all and put on a show of being completely on board.

"My saving grace was our Partner Manager, Jake Zuniga. He had been doing the job for 9 years in its many iterations, knew the customers and the vendors and the solutions. He also knew how to talk me off the ledge thanks to his perseverance in this business.

"He'd always say 'Whatever it is around this place, good or bad, won't last; so, don't get too comfortable or too upset about anything.' It was stellar advice.

"It's amazing how much I would do differently if I had it to do again, but I certainly learned a considerable amount just by going out and doing. I took solace in the fact most of these customers said they had never heard from Majestech-Ware or CTMI unless we wanted their money – trying to sell something or trying to do a renewal.

"Lots of the folks I talked to already had some level of investment with us, and I took the approach that I'd rather bring more value to the existing contract or resources they were entitled to out of the gates. I wanted to prove my worth first, be responsive and deliver. It's what I did in my previous Majestech-Ware role when I had no idea what I was doing. Believe me, this gig had an even steeper learning curve.

"I remember being on these highly technical calls and listening to these specialists rattle off stuff about code and infrastructure specifications and I had no idea what they were talking about. You know what I did? I type 104 words per minute and I wrote down practically every word that was said. I didn't understand much of anything, but my recap e-mails impressed people with their thoroughness so at least I was effective. It wasn't until about 6 months in when the words I wrote started making any sense to me at all. But I could regurgitate my notes on subsequent calls and project confidence.

"I was running too fast to slow down. The nice thing is I started all of these great conversations and then I'd hand the leads I created off to the account team and vendors so I could move on and prospect more. Trouble is, they did nothing with these opportunities, and it left me spinning my wheels.

"I did, however, personally prospect and close the largest deal in our organization that year."

"No kidding?!" I exclaimed. "How did that come about?"

"Keep in mind, I've worked one-call close sales cycles in the telecom business. I worked one-call close sales cycles in the advertising business. There were exceptions, but that was true of the majority of our deals. My time overseeing retail teams was about the same – you'd close the deal while you had them shopping around or you likely did not at all.

"CTMI's data, collaboration and hardware products don't sell themselves and often involve demos, robust planning sessions and articulate strategy for implementation and training. It was a whole new world for my selling style and perspective.

"It wasn't until one of our first regional leadership meetings until I was briefed on the extensive list of tools we had at our disposal - I was about six weeks in. One of the reports showed any customer – sometimes company names, sometimes just a person's name or e-mail address – who had exhibited any usage at all of our CTMI data and AI solution. It could have been the most basic of trials, it could have been a free demo. Anyhow, if there was one thing I learned as a player-coach starting a book of business in the hardware space, it was to run at scale and create a community around what I was doing to cover up the fact I had no idea what I was doing. I didn't need to have a clue to get a conversation."

I chuckled.

"With the report, I used whatever information I had to go on and took it to social media. Thanks mostly to LinkedIn, I found the company and sent very personalized connection requests to as many pertinent people at each organization I could find. For one in particular – a gym management software start-up named FitSmart – I targeted 30 senior and IT leaders of their 100+ employees. 11 accepted my connection request and 1 responded to my follow-up note days later.

"In it, I took the approach that I was connecting because they were investing in our services today and I'd love to introduce their CTMI resources along with support they were entitled to. Who would say no to that, right?"

"I love it," I replied, mesmerized by this line of thinking. "What made you think of that?"

"Everyone I was talking to was tired of rarely hearing from us and when they did it was to renew a contract or trying to sell them something new," I asked. "If I showed them value on top of what they were already getting, the probability of them accepting my request and subsequent meeting requests was heightened. Sales is all about probability and odds. And anything you can do to increase your chances at every step of the sales cycle, the better your chance of eventually earning the business."

"Brilliant," I marveled. "So, this approach worked?"

"It worked unbelievably," Vincent replied.

The 1 responder from FitSmart pointed Vincent to someone else at the company – Shane Bright – to whom Vincent's team had actually sold hardware while he was in his previous role! They had sold to 8,000 unique customers during his 8 quarters in role, so Vincent came across many similar folks in the time to come.

"No matter how many times I go out on a sales call, you'd think I would have known by now to have no pre-conceived notions whatsoever," Vincent recalled. "I took a vendor out there with me and literally thought we'd sign a small $25,000 deal or so and be done with it in the room. I was very wrong. Thankfully!

"After introductions and surmising what they were trying to do, they were weighing us against three other vendors. They were looking to do predictive analytics based on predicting churn – of their members and of their client's gyms. It was a fantastic use case. There were several layers of potential partnership there and in the end, we optimized their website, their financial reporting, their data platform and set up machine learning tools. It was the biggest net new deal in the organization that year. And it introduced a whole new offering FitSmart was able to offer to potential new clubs that inherently utilized our platform.

"Thing of the matter is no one else was translating these reports we had access to into new social connections and then into deals. I did it 11 times that year alone – found folks via social platforms based on obscure reports I had stumbled upon and instead of focusing on 1 or 2 people in these organizations who could easily ignore me, I'd target 30 to 50. I used the reports, cast a really wide net, developed relationships in new organizations and got deals done.

"It was so easy to replicate those efforts, frankly. Sure, I'd personalize the note specific to the business and the reason I was reaching out, and I'd do some copy and paste. But I'd add their name, send the personal request and then I'd follow up with another personalized request as to why I was reaching out.

"If I can reach out to 100 people, even if it just gets me one meeting that might eventually lead to a deal, I'll do it. Because I know what I can do with that one meeting."

This was the stuff I loved listening to. Vincent always managed to find and understand the variables at play in every job he did. He would use all variables at his disposal to rewrite the job and become the best who had ever done it.

"So, I'm guessing you had a banner year?" I asked.

It was a weird position for me; knowing much of Vincent's career up to this point, but not really knowing much at all from the past 5 years. That said, he was always successful beyond imagination, so I figured this situation was no different.

"No," Vincent said slowly, shaking his head. "No, it was quite unpleasant."

"How so? Quintana?"

"Yes, that was part of it. A big part," Vincent replied. "I also missed a goal for the first time in my life."

Chapter 2 – Commiserating Over Breakfast

That last line was quite a blow. Certainly, even Michael Jordan once scored 6 points in the second-to-last season of his career in a game against the Indiana Pacers – his lowest career point total. Of course, he bounced back with 51 in the next game against the Charlotte Hornets. And that was at the end of his career. Vincent's career had been storied but he still had a long way to go – at least if I had anything to say about it!

Vincent Scott was not the type of guy who missed a goal; he made it happen no matter what and no matter what cost to himself personally. That said, I had also never seen Vincent look tired or show any signs of aging or lack of jubilant energy even if or when it was just a show.

"I don't believe it," I said. "But this is something I've got to hear."

"Oh, you will," Vincent said. He was clearly reaching back; gearing up to reveal a tale that was quite personal to him.

We were just midway through the meal. The waiter came and refilled our beverages. I had mirrored Vincent's order and it was quite delicious.

Vincent had always enjoyed a good breakfast, akin to his literary heroes Sherlock Holmes and James Bond. Generous eggs, a meat, and a biscuit of some kind were essential to satisfying his palate.

"In hindsight, I spent so much time trying to get every single deal I could. More time than I should have on deals that were relatively small potatoes like $75K, $100K. It took such an act of congress to get just about any deal done based on the rigmarole we'd have to go through like getting pricing, applying incentives, drafting the agreement, any amendments, and getting various people along the way to do their job in a timely fashion.

"Understanding those milestones by making mistakes and missing some along the way by being oblivious to them was the only way – unfortunately – that I learned any of it. All I got from Quintana was guff over the deals – not any type of help or instruction over the steps required.

"It's a shame when you sign more new logos than anyone else in the business *by far* and you are not well regarded by your boss. You're talked down to like you're a problem. And even though very few people hit goal, that didn't make it sting any less.

"It was kind of a perfect storm. I liken it to when I found out Abby was pregnant with Elizabeth – I was in line for promotion, we moved to a new place and there was a lot going on. This was like that on steroids: Abby was pregnant again. October 1, I put a bid on a house and literally got the first house we looked at. So, we were moving. Which, honestly, was a bit of a bummer for me because I loved the apartment we had been in for the last year. But it was cramped as it was and there's no way we could have a family of four in it. Plus, most every deal I had conjured up was dragging out.

"And because the territory hadn't hit goal in 5 years, there was a massive forecast gap that I was absolutely, furiously whittling away at. Quintana's response? *Daily* 7:30 AM conference calls with me to dive into my $2.1 million forecasted gap. It was unheard of.

"So, it was during this time that I developed pretty good relationships with a couple of my top services vendors. One of them was Accord Business Group; I had met them a few years prior when I connected with their Senior Partner on LinkedIn, met him and almost went to work for them. They job offered me then, and I declined to take it at the time, but I hate disappointing people and did not want to leave them empty-handed. So, I gave them Nick Aragon.

"We had worked together at Tel-Cell – though I did not really know him well there. He also came on board at Majestech-Ware as one of our business managers, which is where I got to know him better. He should have gotten my old job when I got promoted and was salty because he didn't; so, I got him the interview and endorsed him for the role at ABG and he got it.

"The other vendor trying to make a name for themselves in the Twin Cities was Merit Productivity. Nick replaced Mick Logan at Accord when he left to go work for Merit. They were likely bigger in Wisconsin up to that point and were growing, so they sold Mick on 'opening the market' in the Twin Cities. They offered him more money. It was a no-brainer.

"The reason this is most relevant is that during this time I got pretty close with both Nick and Mick. Nick was looking for meetings and leads, and my prospecting ability got us in a ton of doors. We came in under the banner of complimentary training and workshops and got just about every meeting I wanted.

Mick, on the other hand, was one of the most diligent networkers I've ever met. He was looking to work with me wherever he could.

"Nick was getting married that December and he and his fiancé and two kids spent a good amount of time with Abby, Elizabeth and me. He knew of my displeasure with Quintana. He also knew of my displeasure with Majestech-Ware as a whole, since they had put me through the ringer in my last job and now with CTMI things weren't much better. I was being micromanaged and being relegated to an administrative pipeline manager role as opposed to that of my pedigree as a decorated sales leader. Because of Nick's prodding – both within Accord and his overtures to me – Accord was making another play to land me.

"Mick had a coffee with Quintana, and she admitted being harder on me than anyone else. Apparently, it was because she knew I was the best and because I had so much potential.

"But that certainly wasn't what I was seeing from her. She did not compliment me. She did not let up on me. She did nothing to help me. All I got from her was 'what you're doing isn't working' as I closed far more net new logos than anyone else, which made her credibility with me nil. But, credibility or not, she was my boss, giving her an exclusive ability to make my life miserable.

"Ironically, she was giving me stretch assignments, but not the stuff that I was strong with like prospecting, growing relationships and leading teams. She wanted me to spend time making presentations on daily scheduling and rhythm of business and another on growing consumption of our product offerings with existing clients.

"I accepted them, because I typically accept every request made of me in hopes it gets me ahead, but in this case it did nothing to bolster my standing with Quintana or anyone else. I suppose it was to force me to get better at the things she thought I did ineffectively, but it did nothing to really help me gain better footing with her.

"I felt like I was drowning. I was doing everything I could to be in every meeting – to be a client advocate, to put in my two cents about how we could support our vendors, and to show Quintana how much and how hard I was working because she was breathing down my neck on an hourly basis.

"We started our day together with those mandatory 7:30 AM calls and she would message me throughout the day no matter what I was doing expecting immediate responses about individual deals. 'Where is this deal?' 'Do you have a formal close plan for this deal – where is it?' I was driving new relationships and forming partnerships and she was stopping me dead in my tracks *every hour* with some kind of minutiae and administrative demand.

"You can't drive the *magnitude* of new deals I was driving and have an elaborate, extremely detailed and milestone-laden full presentation for every single one of them. My approach didn't mix with hers. And no matter how respectful I attempted to be when she imposed her will on me, it wasn't working.

"To be fair, I understand how important it is to have a pipeline and forecast, specifically when you're accountable to shareholders. But I couldn't get any momentum because she was killing it by questioning *everything*. And I was over 100% to goal fiscal year-to-date. Our fiscal year ran July to June, so the first half of our year I was over budget. With no training or really much comprehension of what I was doing.

"Furthermore, she was actually quite counterproductive on deals. We had an account move their headquarters to St. Paul earlier in 2016 – a holding company called OV Group. They were mis-aligned geographically and when the change was made, they were pushed down a notch into our SMB patch even though they were 10,000 employees. Regardless of that, I didn't want to punish the customer for our mistake and my team continued to help them.

"I had it on Quintana's radar because they belonged in our territory and everyone agreed on that fact, and she committed to getting it fixed so this rolled up to my team. A couple of months later as the deal neared closure, she said she was not going to agree to approve or help get approved OV Group coming to our patch. She claimed she had an issue with another account of that size coming into our patch while we had such a massive gap in pipeline because we would take on more quota.

"I had to stop and drop everything to write up the business case showing how we would net an additional $2 *million* in revenue *on top of the quota* we were taking. The deal closed and she did nothing with it. *That one deal would have put me over quota for the year.* I am the one who did the deal. Somebody got a $20,000 bonus for a deal they had nothing to do with that my team constructed. Disgusting."

Vincent shook his head, clearly still perturbed and in disbelief over this turn of events.

"How in the world does that even happen?" I gasped. "Wouldn't she have wanted the money?"

"There are a variety of factors," he replied. "First, the money was going to be realized by CTMI no matter what happened. If it stayed in our SMB space, 1 rep gets paid on it and one manager who oversaw that whole division. If *my* team lands the deal, the reps and specialists get paid, I get paid, on up the chain. CTMI paid out far less money in commission because of that deal not getting assigned properly to the team who actually closed it. And as far as I know, Quintana attached her name to it anyway and Floyd Irving paid her.

"I've come to realize that in a big company, there's a lot of bureaucracy and politics and different cooks in the kitchen. Sometimes too many. So many people ready to touch your deal and take credit but very few who actually want to do any work. Quintana knew she had no chance of hitting goal, so she decided pretty quickly she was going to crack down on us as best she could and show her boss that *we* were the problem. She decided I was her biggest problem."

"They knew who you were, right?" I managed, in disbelief. "I mean, they know you are *the* Vincent Scott?"

He managed to laugh a bit at that, however I could tell it had not been a particularly funny or fun time in his work history.

"I don't play up who I am and what I've done, but certainly they see my posts and blogs and articles that go out. They know of my books. They knew I had been a VP and Director. But I think that makes you a target in certain situations. CTMI was heading in a different direction with their business and claiming to be a 'productivity business fueled by empathy.' It felt like anything but.

"I believed in the CEO and his vision, but my immediate chain of command was a complete joke."

Vincent paused. This was utterly fascinating. Amazing to see the trials and tribulations this man continued to encounter in spite of his talents and contributions and successes. He had come up against someone who didn't care at all who he was or what he could do; they were actually hell-bent on taking him out instead.

"On the one hand, I've finally got my wife and my kid full time, plus a house, and I get up every day and drive my dream car Aston Martin to work and sit in an office with a window view. The money was better than anything I ever sniffed at ABM when I thought I was on top of the world. And I was able to infuse my unique flair into the role – doing events and webinars with these vendors and my technical specialists that no one else had ever done. I led the division in new customer acquisitions. But I was being stifled and kicked at every turn.

"And it just kept getting worse. Quintana challenged me on the forecasting of a deal with one of our global organizations. A lot of their licensing fell overseas, and no one ever thought to tell me how the revenue counted for us when we signed deals including overseas revenue.

"So, of course, when the deal hit the revenue was off. Not by a lot – relatively – on the $5 million deal. Off by a couple hundred grand. She read me the Riot Act.

"She accused me *over* and *over* of making a mistake forecasting and that I had a *serious* forecasting problem in general, which was way off base.

"While I learned long ago to just keep my mouth shut when I vehemently disagreed with bad managers, I couldn't keep quiet. Not this time – not after all of the targeting she had already done against me.

"I disagreed verbally to her face, and then asked why she nor anyone else had ever shared this information. Turns out, she didn't even know how foreign licensing paid out. And as a result of that situation, she documented a meeting with me where she 'covered the expected basic competencies' of my job with me. I kid you not.

"Quintana pulled up my job description and had me read it and sign a document acknowledging what my job competencies were. I don't know that I have ever been more insulted in my life.

"Between that, the OV Group deal she screwed me out of, the daily 7:30 calls... I was *frozen* with anger. I was petrified. And the old me – the ABM me – I wouldn't have stood for it. I would have gone toe to toe with her and undermined her... taken it up over her head and shouted her incompetence from the rooftops. I would have gone to HR, would have led a coup of other dissatisfied workers against her. And probably gotten fired.

"Somehow, I kept my cool."

He paused for a sip of his water before continuing.

"When my friend Emily died suddenly in a car accident in 2015, it changed everything about how I lived my life," Vincent reflected. "I started living day by day; sometimes moment by moment. Just slowing it down to get through. It wasn't easy, but I fought through these brutal days under Quintana with no real end in sight – other than the potential of going to ABG – by focusing moment by moment.

"I felt trapped. The money and benefits were good, and I had a kid on the way and a new house. Sure, I made a boatload off the large deal from the hardware division, but taxes and Jamaica took a pretty big chunk out of it. Plus, I was stashing away money to send my kids to college.

"I responded by dropping my stance on ultra-conservative forecasting, and basically created opportunities in our pipeline with just about every customer who had indicated any interest in anything – marking them as potential upside deals, but closing the 'gap' Quintana kept harping about. I was so enraged while I did it, but it had to be done. I basically did it out of pure spite.

"It got her off my back about *that*, but then it was always something else. Like my attention to job competencies. I had even pointed out how committed I was to CTMI because I had gotten opportunities to work with partners for higher base salary and turned them down. Quintana actually asked me why *wouldn't* I leave to go work for a vendor. She did not hide her dislike of me or desire to have me leave.

"I just feel like there's no loyalty. Sure, I was a rogue and a pain at ABM, but they *broke the law* to take me out with something completely unfounded. I was sure as heck praised at Cellular Horizons and Tel-Cell when I took those markets from worst to first and then I was exiled after I bucked their system. I took a risk to leave Tel-Cell for a consultant firm that flat-out lied to me. And then my boss at Majestech-Ware did everything he could to unseat me from the global #1 spot every quarter for 2 years and he failed. He promised me a promotion he created for me... and then gave it to someone else.

"I've worked with 103-degree fever. I've hobbled into work hunched over barely able to walk after hurting my back. I've done nights, weekends, and regular 60, 70-hour weeks. I took off *one week* of vacation when my first kid was born. I've given *everything* to my career and yet I am still treated like I'm nothing special. Like I'm inferior and should be grateful just to have a job. In fact, I'm treated far worse than mediocre performers or performers who luck into success because they have a large deal fall into their lap.

"The coolest thing about my books even though I haven't sold enough to retire is that I've met people all over the world. I've been interviewed on dozens of podcasts. And these hosts *marvel* that I still carry the bag; I still sell, where most

31

other 'gurus' don't. They are blown away by it. And the more I endure, the more blown away I am, too – that it hasn't broken me completely. That after everything I've been through, I still have any motivation or desire left to compete."

Vincent paused again before stating, "Every day was absolutely brutal. Sure, I was closing these new logos on relatively smaller deals to get them reclassified from non-managed SMB to our mid-size group. Then I'd have our Large Business Group try to justify taking one of my team's accounts because of an acquisition by a company in another geography, even though all of the decisions were still being made in the Twin Cities. Then I had our Government team try to justify taking one of our top accounts *just because* they were doing a fraction of their work with the government.

"To add insult to injury, my first job in high school and college was with Cooke's Grocery Store in Mankato. Even the parent company ditched CTMI/Majestech-Ware on my watch in a really nasty way. Nothing I could have done about it at all, but I had to take the blame from Quintana."

"How was Quintana *supporting* you?"

Vincent laughed, but not in a way that he thought it was comical.

"That's the best part," he scoffed. "I was supposed to have a meeting one day with Cooke's senior leadership as we were trying to hammer out a deal, and she sent in one of my peers *from Wisconsin* to handle the meeting! She called me while I was driving there to tell me I wasn't needed!

"What an utter vote of no confidence. Rather than trying to help or support or even doing anything at all to make the situation better, she just sent in one of my peers for this critical meeting. No explanation. No communication. No teaching moment. Any good manager would have gone to the meeting *with* me given the circumstances. She didn't even get involved or participate in any way to help me – she just replaced me with someone who had been in the job longer. We lost the business anyway."

"Oh, my goodness," I gasped. "What did you do?"

"I know what you're thinking," Vincent said, setting down his coffee. "The old Vincent Scott wouldn't have put up with it. That's when he would have gone *beyond* hitting the roof.

"But I didn't. I expressed that I was surprised to learn I was not going to the meeting. I expressed that I wish I had known. Her response was 'I'm telling you now,' and then she changed the subject back to 'gap' in other areas that would have been eradicated had she kept her word and allowed me to sign OV Group.

"I realized – more and more – that I just had to keep my head down and mouth shut. She was *obsessed* with destroying me and it was abundantly clear I couldn't do anything about it. I could only hurt myself if I spoke up.

"Quintana had moved her family from Mexico to Minneapolis for this job, so she sure wasn't going anywhere. It made ABG look all the better as a personal escape plan, and those conversations continued but they seemed to be dragging their feet. I expected an offer in October, then November, and then it sounded like closer to first of the year. All the while, I still wanted to stick around CTMI the longer it took because of bonuses I had earned and because my upcoming paternity leave would transpire in March 2017. The closer it got to that date, the less it made sense to leave.

"I became a scapegoat for everything going wrong. Rather than being heralded for these incredible wins – like FitSmart and others that came about out of thin air and social selling – Quintana would rake me over the coals every chance she got.

"She blasted me once when an executive briefing my team set up didn't have breakfast or lunch booked, when I had literally nothing to do with that process whatsoever and the receptionist had dropped the ball. I'd catch flak for not reporting that Cooke's had a competitive threat early enough, even though I reported it the day I found out. Not forecasting enough or forecasting too much. Just getting hammered on the details of everything – so much to the point I was paralyzed sometimes to even do my job.

"Quintana's boss, John Deever – who worked directly for Floyd Irving, actually left around this time. Along with his General Manager equivalent in the Large Business Group – Matt Rockwell – they formed their own services vendor specific to data and analytics. I was fascinated, honestly, how many people turned over between the old Majestech-Ware and the new CTMI – these guys had been there 15 years together and now they were gone.

"It made leaving corporate for the vendor path look even more attractive, frankly. These seasoned vets were leaving to start their own vendors rather than staying at CTMI under this new, terrible leadership. But the offer from Accord did not come when I expected it and so I had no choice but to just kept plowing along.

"We got a new General Manager, Jordan Waters, and I really liked his energy and enthusiasm. Like everyone, though, it remained to be seen if he was legitimate or just another hyped up flake.

"He had a great reputation. Most people I talked to indicated that this was a positive change. The year prior, he had won CTMI Manager of the Year. I liked his sports analogies. But as long as I worked for Quintana, I knew she would poison any boss of hers against me. I felt defeated.

"I do have to say – I liked my team. I met Lucy Burke, Charlotte Baines and Stu Sanders and did hit it off. They covered Wisconsin, Iowa, and North Dakota, respectively. South Dakota had been covered by a colleague who left for a competitor.

"We were able to collectively vent about the frustrations of the role and what it had become, plus the antics of Quintana. One thing we all agreed on was that she was hardest on me.

"She'd tell me I was not open enough with my business, even though I invited her to client and partner meetings on a daily basis and she had full visibility to my schedule – and she'd never show. She told me I wouldn't take coaching, but the only example she'd point out when I politely asked for an example was when I was told adamantly that I made a mistake when I forecasted overseas licensing without any guidance on how to do so.

"I literally started making it a point to say 'Thank you for the coaching' during *every* discussion, e-mail or IM conversation with her. She likely either thought I meant it or that I was being a jerk. Likely the latter.

"I had teammates that I could vent to, but none of them were in town. Our partner manager, Jake Zuniga – or 'Z' as we called him – was in the Twin Cities. He was the most effective in talking me down when I became so frustrated I was ready to bail. He was the only one with whom I shared full transparency – the ABG discussions and potential offer, all of the frustrations with Quintana, and basically most roadblocks I experienced with our programs and vendors. You know, the stuff Quintana should have been helping me with.

"Z would take me out for drinks or pizza at this bar down the street from our office and give me some perspective. Having been there a decade and seeing the changes and revolving door of managers and direction had given him a good vantage point. It was helpful. It was just what I needed to hear.

"Z was one of the first people I met when I started with Majestech-Ware and we officially worked together when I took my new role with CTMI. He was accountable for the full territory that Quintana oversaw from a vendor perspective. It was his responsibility to work with the territory managers to ensure the funding and vendor programs were leveraged – that we had folks internally and with vendors working with customers to scope, proof out and execute on our solution.

"He was also a Dad – 8 years older than me, with four kids. We spoke every day. He was very well known in the industry and community. Probably the only guy I could relate to. And, as 'luck' would have it, he also had gotten a new manager – Kandace Newman – who was trying to run him out of the business just like Quintana was doing to me. Brave new world.

"He would tell me I was doing great and that I was the hardest working guy he'd ever met. That I had my act together better in 9 months than people who had been doing it for years. Z had worked with 5 of my predecessors in market and dozens of folks regionally who had done my role, so I took it as high praise. It was stuff I needed to hear from someone to have any semblance of confidence, but it didn't make the day-to-day beatings much easier to endure.

"On top of that, in December, my wife Abby went on bedrest during her pregnancy with our second kid and was unable to work. It could obviously have been much worse and overall she was OK and the baby was OK, but it was just more stress for us all. Instability at work and supporting the family solo was not a great mix. The ABG offer was nowhere to be found and time kept on slipping into 2017 which was guaranteed to be an interesting year in its own right.

"Quintana continued her antics – I was working another deal based on a merger that transpired with a company in Illinois. The Illinois team got a whiff of what was brewing and started trying to claim that they were going to sell it under that company's umbrella. Of course, the customer just wanted the best deal, which would have been under the larger organization that my team managed. I raised it to Quintana to help settle any dispute before it happened. She assured me she would ensure it fell in our patch and the customer got what they needed. A week later, after I had already gotten the incentives approved and was near signature, the deal went to Chicago – per Quintana. She told me it was not up for debate.

"She had conducted conversations presumably with her peer in that market, excluding me, not keeping me in the loop and certainly not communicating. I raised the issue and made the obvious case for the deal to reside in our territory. She didn't even get paid on the deal with it going to her peer. But she didn't care. Anything she could do to hurt me, she'd do it. It made no sense.

"A new program started about that time. 'Data Days.' We were supposed to prospect and tee up conversations for our technical specialists, whereby we would introduce them and drive pipeline for the team – it was a mandate from above. I personally drove the most of these engagements *in the entire company* and after listening to our technical specialist on a couple of calls started leading them *by myself*.

"My tech lead was amazed. Quintana couldn't have cared less. I offered to share best practices of how I was driving these conversations and this pipeline, and she never replied.

"About that time, Quintana also became very preoccupied with me creating an extremely elaborate paternity leave plan, assigning tasks and milestones for every weekly call and every deal to other members of the team – including her. We would have a call every week until March to gauge my progress of this paternity leave plan. Remember me telling you this because it becomes pertinent later.

"Also, in that category, Quintana went with me to a customer meeting for the first and only time in February 2017; it was another SMB deal I had prospected. I led the meeting. She went rambling on about something completely irrelevant, as she had a tendency to do – partners used to make fun of her all the time for her long-winded spiels about nothing. Anyhow, she told me that I 'did a great job leading the meeting' and that my 'value story was tremendous.'"

"Wow - a compliment!" I raved. "You must have been thrilled."

"I thought it was a turning point, especially after what we had been through. I thought we had another one when her car wouldn't start on a really bad winter snow day. I stayed with her until her husband could arrive to pick her up. She seemed very thankful because she was scared; being from Mexico, she had never been in a snowstorm like that much less seen much snow."

"A very Christian thing of you to do," I marveled.

"You know, I think you see people's true colors in unexpected circumstances. How they react when they're not in control says a lot about them. She was just terrified.

"I started operating as if the ABG offer was never coming. It was stretching closer to paternity leave and I had a solid quarterly bonus that would soon be due to me, so it made no sense to leave anyhow. Nick Aragon told me they were now thinking of trying to get me in May when I got back from paternity leave. Fair enough – get a nice paycheck and time off with family, come back and make a move.

"That was another interesting caveat – CTMI gives guys 3 months of paternity leave. 3 months! Can you believe it? When Elizabeth was born, my tyrant boss at the time Keith Dickhauser asked me, 'You're not taking any time off, are you?'

"I had to take a week of vacation time just to have any time off with Abby and the baby. And now I had 3 months. But instead of taking 3 months which would have taken me to the end of the fiscal year, I decided to come back in half that time on May 1 because I had 11 deals I needed to close."

"That's dedication," I marveled again. "Very selfless. How did Abby feel about that?"

"She understood. Besides, after a few weeks, I would have just been in the way anyway. She didn't need me there all the time after April.

"And irony of ironies, it was February 2017 when I saw Keith Dickhauser for the first time in 7 years."

This was a profound statement.

Keith Dickhauser had interviewed and eventually hired Vincent Scott as a Senior Manager in the ABM Advertising Bureau in March 2006. That began a chain reaction that resulted in Vincent meeting his wife, Vincent's promotion a year later to Director, 2 years at the helm of a division that expanded to three states and 220 people, and eventually a dizzying story of investigation and betrayal and revenge when Keith illegally eliminated Vincent's role and railroaded his career.

It took over 3 years for the court battle to conclude and Vincent's life had never been the same.

Vincent took a sip of his water. His meal was nearly concluded. I dared not speak at this moment.

"I didn't know if he saw me or not, and it's even more ironic because I was there to meet with Ben Schwartz, the CEO of one of customers regarding a million-dollar deal we were putting together for his document software company. After walking through the door of the Oceanaire Seafood Room, I glanced left and there Keith was – interviewing someone for a job.

"Ben walked toward me from the other direction just moments later, and I was swept up into that conversation. A part of me wanted to say something to Keith, but the moment was over and I went to my lunch and to work on this deal. I thought about it during the entire lunch. He was gone when we left."

I did not speak right away.

"I've got to ask," I began, "How did it feel?"

"I didn't know if I'd ever see him again," Vincent replied after a moment's hesitation. "I've seen *most* of the players from that saga again. Not all. I've seen a few at coffee shops or on the streets downtown and we did not exchange words. My old reps and some of the managers – especially after I won the lawsuit – started crawling back for the most part; many of them wanting jobs. Many of us are connected on social media.

"Some of the senior leaders I never spoke to again. It felt surreal, I suppose. Being at a completely different place in life and seeing the guy that was so instrumental in my career at that point.

"I look back sometimes and trace it all back to that firing. I spent so many years just trying to equal or surpass where I felt like I was or should have been. I still think about it regularly. Almost every day. What could I have done differently; what I should have done differently. I don't regret standing up to him – he was breaking the law. But I was out of control and I believed the managers and reps working for me were my friends, and I was dead wrong. I learned a lesson the very hard way and it shaped everything I've done since personally and professionally.

"If I hadn't gotten fired, I never would have finished my book and gotten it published. It was only because of my book that Jordan Wallace's wife flagged my résumé and gave it to him, which is how I wound up at Cellular Horizons. Because of Cellular Horizons, I followed Saul Portman to Tel-Cell. Then I met Mitch Finkleson at Tel-Cell and even though I made a poor decision to move to a defunct consultant firm that sold me a bill of goods, I wound up being recruited by Majestech-Ware because of him. Ironically, Tel-Cell had filed suit against him for recruiting so many folks from Tel-Cell and had I not gone to the consultant firm, I could never have made that move. That led me to CTMI."

"Is that a good thing?" I asked, half-jokingly.

"I'm getting there," Vincent reciprocated with a wry smile. "I joined Majestech-Ware out of necessity and with a very 'sixth-man' approach. I knew I was coming in as a contributor, not expecting much out of myself. I viewed it like Michael Jordan playing for the Wizards at age 40 – I was going to be a role player who hopefully could contribute in some unique way.

"Surprisingly, for me anyway, things took off for me at Majestech-Ware. Slowly but surely, and when they did, they went off like a rocket.

"Also surprisingly, I was taken aback by just how much effort managers in the division tried to stifle me or change rules to keep me down. Then I finally felt like I broke through by getting the infamous hardware deal and the VP role, only to have my world change again. I pivoted into this Territory Manager gig and was again surprised at how much I felt like I had to battle management daily rather than be empowered or helped in any way.

"Everything pertinent to driving engagements or initiatives or workshops – I led the organization in. But Quintana told me I had too much going on – even though it was the company throwing us these different initiatives every day. 'Drive this initiative, now this one, now this one.' She only reiterated I 'had to hit the number' but of course her blocking me on the OV Group deal I *created* made it clear she didn't want me to hit my number. She purposely targeted me and tried to destroy my career.

"I did keep in touch with Miranda Bond; keeping her apprised of what was going on. She took the buyout and severance when the merger happened and went to another of our vendors at a senior capacity. What a different perspective she had; certainly not the direction that my business unit seemed to be taking. But, fortunately for me, having been maliciously silenced and eliminated by ABM once upon a time and the whirlwind since with every company I had worked for, I knew I had to keep my mouth shut and head down and do what I was told even when it made zero sense.

"It was an abyss that was easy to be sucked into. It was nothing to do a 12-, 14-, 16-hour day and still feel like you had accomplished relatively nothing. Unfortunately, I had not gotten the benefit of having someone show me how it was done – how to aggressively manage my own schedule. How to say no to a completely pointless meeting or request, because it took me time to figure out which ones had value.

"Every vendor would try to manage me and get me to do their work for them. There were rampant customer support issues with CTMI, and I'd get sucked into those if I wasn't careful. I came to realize that no specialist and no vendor was truly going to drive momentum or a deal forward, so if I wanted it done, I had to do it myself.

"And it was time consuming. I had two major problems – I allowed myself to get pulled into everything regardless of the deal size and I needed to more aggressively manage my day.

"Of all the things I can say about Quintana, we did *eventually* have one conversation that stuck with me in a positive way. She looked at my calendar with me and challenged me to look at every meeting in a given day and ask myself if it really was prioritized properly; if it was something that had to transpire today, or was I allowing a meeting that could wait to take precedent over something more important. She was right. I had to get better at moving the pro bono work or the philosophical conversations with vendors who weren't actually doing anything in my territory down or potentially out. Given enough time in role, I could eventually look back and realize – based on track record – which vendors were worth my time and which were just looking for a handout.

"It was hard enough to manage forecasting, corral the deals that were out there, conduct vendor discussions, prospect, deal with the 'scored marketing leads' that were a pile of crap, file numerous administrative reports per week, stay on top of all of the support issues, respond to a dozen redundant messages from Quintana throughout the day, manually write up hours of additional reporting when we had automated tools that were supposed to do it for us and construct a robust manual paternity leave plan.

"On top of that, I was getting up at 3:30 or 4 to work out and trying to be a husband and a Dad. At one point I fell asleep momentarily on the treadmill and banged up my shin before catching myself. I was a disaster.

"It's funny, because I vividly remember when I lost my job at ABM – I went from nonstop calls and demands and people pulling on me constantly to absolutely nothing. Dead silence. Now, I had once again created this engine of fever pitch; I was marketing for the partners and their solutions, trying to drive discussions, responding to things left and right. Because I was so proactive marketing for partners and others weren't, partners took advantage of me and they contacted me all the time. I did everything I could to respond. It, along with everything else, created a vicious cycle.

"I had to learn that if I didn't answer a non-critical question, they'd get the answer somewhere else. That took me a long time to reconcile, considering I had developed such a strong reputation based on my responsiveness and ability to get the answer to everything. It was a dangerous Catch-22.

"Everything was so political, too. Because I oversaw the territory, you'd have customers and partners who wanted to keep you at arm's length. You'd have partners who tried to do their own thing without you. But the second you tried to introduce a strategy or a vendor for anything anywhere, everybody'd be up in arms. The partners that would never respond when you tried to get feedback or work together sure got in a tizzy the second you talked to 'their' customer or introduced any other vendor or way of thinking.

"Because of that, I was *very* often the bad guy. Which I made light of in conversation, but the truth is it takes its toll. It's not fun being vilified by partners and customers alike on a regular basis while your boss makes clear you're her least favorite person on earth and you feel like you're just spinning your wheels all day every day and it's going nowhere. Especially, when once upon a time, you were well regarded and going somewhere with your career.

"I actually logged onto a call a few minutes late once because I was back-to-back all day and the partner was talking bad about me thinking I wasn't there. They were saying they went to me for support and a discount and I turned them down. I patiently listened, then corrected them when they were finished as all I had done was send back some clarifying questions so I could best frame the ask internally to the powers that be. I didn't just blindly take their request and try to spoon-feed them what they wanted; I did my job. They were, of course, aghast that I had caught them bad-mouthing me, and attempted to cover it up, but it didn't matter. It was just another pain point I had to take and shove under the rug so I could make it through the day. For me, it was just about survival. It really always is.

"At least it wasn't like ABM where those folks acted like I was family and we spent birthdays and kids' birthdays and holidays together and then they abandoned me completely and wouldn't even speak to me at my darkest hour. At least these people make clear their priorities and that all they care about is themselves.

"But there is a strength in learning and understanding that someone is only out for themselves. It empowers you to turn every conversation with them into one where you are making some sort of a deal – you're positioning something that helps them as a milestone on the way to you getting what you want. If you can overtly frame every scenario for which you want their buy-in with how *they* win, you can get what you want every time."

"That is literal gold," I remarked.

"And it's something most people don't get," he continued. "Many people just try to recommend to customers and partners or specialists a certain course of action and throw in a couple of reasons why. But if the reasons are not personal to your audience, there is little chance they'll walk with you where you want to take them. But if you focus on making it about them – whatever it is – they will very willingly come along for the ride."

"So, I have to ask, you're not friends with anyone from ABM anymore?"

"No," Vincent said quickly and dispassionately. "I'm connected with many of them on social media and I've seen a couple of them over the years, but there's no close friendships anymore. I'm friendly with some of them, but for various reasons even those are folks either I've drifted from or they've drifted from me."

"Interesting," I commented. "Specifically, as you said, as close as it seemed you were to so many. How does that make you feel?"

"It doesn't," he answered quickly again, shrugging his shoulders. "It was such a long time ago. I don't think about it."

I wasn't quite sure I fully believed him, but was not going to press him on the point.

The waiter came and left the check. Vincent graciously picked it up before I had the chance; he had a knack for that.

"So - Sydney?" I prompted. Vincent, who had spent the majority of the breakfast conversation sullenly relating events, suddenly smiled and his face lit up.

"She's amazing," Vincent replied. "So talkative, so cute, so entertaining and so smart. She's curious. She's very particular and opinionated. Not sure where she got any of that from." Vincent laughed.

42

We rose from the table and walked toward the door.

Because I had utilized taxis while in Minneapolis, Vincent was going to chauffeur me for the day before dropping me off at the airport.

We exited the restaurant, and entered the lot, walking toward his black Aston Martin DB7 convertible. I smiled. "How long have you had this ride again?"

"Six years," Vincent responded. "I bought it when I was certain I'd be a bachelor forever." He laughed, and I followed suit.

"Yeah, how did that turn out?"

"The way it was supposed to."

Chapter 3 – Eleven Deals and a Baby

"It was Thursday, March 17 at about 8:45 in the morning and I was just about to leave for the office so I could finish some trainings and take calls. Sydney was due in two days, so I was near the wrap-up time, but there's always so much to do. I was planning to have lunch with Jake Zuniga.

"And then Abby shouted down the laundry chute, 'Babe! BABE!' and her tone caught me off guard. She said her water broke. She was really excited. I went into laser-focused Daddy mode. She's always the emotional one and I'm the logical, analytical one.

"We grabbed our bags, went out the door and picked up Elizabeth from school before going to the hospital. Our parents got there. It was kind of slow going for a while but in the last couple of hours things seemed to move quickly.

"Sydney arrived at 8:15 PM. 6 pounds, 14 ounces, 20 inches. At first sight, she seemed like a brunette clone of Elizabeth at that same stage – so many similarities in mannerisms. It was surreal. Ironically, now they couldn't act more differently.

"There were early struggles with getting accustomed, lack of sleep, massive shift in routines, etc. But it has worked out. Our family definitely felt more complete. How are your kids?"

I told him. We chatted a bit about the kids and families.

"What's on the itinerary for today?" I asked. We were driving in downtown Minneapolis.

"Well..." Vincent started slowly, "I have to stop by the office for a quick meeting."

"Gotcha." I did not want to pry, figuring if he wanted to tell me what was afoot that he would. It was ambiguous enough it could be anything!

"It was nice because Abby gave me the idea of doing a diaper party prior to Sydney's birth," Vincent continued, ominously changing the subject. "Friends, family, all at the house... we played games, smoked cigars, spent time in my bar, had scotch. And they gave me more diapers and baby clothes than we knew what to do with.

"I tied up loose ends at the office after we got back from the hospital and then I was scheduled off until May. It was a nice reset all around.

"I could have stayed off until almost July, meaning I would have missed the final quarter of our fiscal year. That said, I opted to come back in enough time to finalize the last 11 deals of our year."

"Interesting," I commented. "Do you regret it?"

"In hindsight, yes and no," he said quickly. "Given how my return ultimately went, I should have just taken 3 months. You can't get back any of that priceless time with your family.

"Career-wise, I finished that fiscal year with no regrets. I came back early to get a job done and I did it. Furthermore, I did get more time with Sydney in those six weeks than I had gotten 10 years prior at ABM when Elizabeth was born. I get to see her every day, and I saw Elizabeth half the time for the majority of her first 8 years. It's different. It's better.

"I did a lot of meal prep and diaper changes and everything I could around the house. I went hiking with my father-in-law and went to all of Elizabeth's volleyball practices and games. Played with Abby and the kids, went places, visited family. Much of it was very therapeutic.

"Abby and I both had to go back to work the same week. So, after 6 weeks with both of us off and shedding our old routines, it was back to her working seven nights on, seven nights off at the hospital overnight and me working 12 hour days, trying to work out and being up with Sydney when Abby was gone.

"The time off also made me very focused when I came back. It was good to get back to routines I took for granted, like my 4:30 AM workouts and cadence with my team and driving deals to closure. I came back with 11 deals I had to close, and I closed *every single one of them*."

"Oh, wow," I marveled. "I bet Quintana was happy!"

"You would think, but that's actually when the whole relationship went off the rails."

I gasped. "Are you *kidding* me?"

"I'm afraid not," he said with chagrin. "It took every bit I had to get those 11 deals done. There was one I had haggled for most of the year that the vendor told me they could turn into a million dollars – we closed at $75K. Very frustrating how much time I had to spend on that deal to get that result.

"Another district tried to steal a deal I prospected because they had another office in Wisconsin. I managed to stave that off, with no help at all from Quintana. I closed down deals with a couple more start-up's, but they were also relatively small. I got another big pre-commit from a supply chain software company. It was amazing that I pulled it all off.

"I was also more than a little surprised to find that Quintana had charged me with creating this complex paternity leave plan and no one save Jake Zuniga did *anything* on it while I was gone – Quintana included. She was supposed to conduct weekly calls for my territory during my absence and did none of them. There were numerous actions the extended specialist team was supposed to complete – most of them were left undone and Quintana had done absolutely nothing to tend to these 'critical' items.

"Quintana had also not had my back when a customer complained during my absence and said she thought she could get contract terms that didn't exist. The customer was so desperate she lied and claimed I had told her she could, knowing I wasn't there to defend myself. Rather than have my back or even give me the benefit of the doubt, Quintana said to the customer on a call that she would fully investigate my actions. She mentioned *to the customer* it would be a code of conduct violation. Thankfully, my team stepped in and informed her that I had done nothing wrong. The vendor talked the customer down. It fizzled out. But her attempts to get rid of me knew no bounds.

"She also signed away my largest consuming customer while I was gone, even though I had been successfully fighting the battle to keep them in my territory all year. She had no qualms about reaching out to me while I was on leave asking about 'potential code of conduct issues' rooted in the customer's lie about contract terms, but she sure didn't let me know she got rid of my top customer without saying a word to me.

"This is the one the government team was trying to take because 12% of their business was done with the government. The rest was with commercial customers. I had blocked the government team from taking them *three times*. In my absence, Quintana handed them over – probably gleefully. It plunged me farther down the ranks, because I lost their year-to-date revenue.

"I was 97% to goal year-to-date when I came back May 1. I needed to find another $2M in annual revenue to plug the gap and I was up against time. The deals I closed eradicated some of that gap, but the time lost halted momentum in other areas and no bluebirds came out of the sky.

"I was actually pleasantly surprised to get a perfect quarterly appraisal from Quintana the first week I was back. Despite our differences, the now two quarterly appraisals she had covered with me had been near-flawless.

"At that time, I was also approached about a couple of internal job opportunities – once in the Large Business Group and another in the hardware group – basically the team that absorbed what I had done previously as a Regional Manager at Majestech-Ware. I had been there, done that – but it would give me the chance to escape this dead end working for a boss who clearly and intensely hated me. Things were looking up.

"After a couple of interviews for the Device Manager role, I felt good. The hiring manager loved our conversation. It was general consensus that I was a shoo-in. Then she spoke with Quintana and I never heard from her again.

"The Large Business Group Director, Renee Wilkins, was interested in my candidacy for a role on her team but indicated she had to wait to do anything until July when she'd know the new direction of the business. Things always had a tendency of changing at the onset of a new fiscal year. That was fair enough. She wanted to stay in touch and keep the dialogue warm.

"I did as much as I could to finish out the fiscal year. It was not a full year in role, and while I had been #2 on Quintana's team prior to going on paternity leave I dipped to #4 and 93% to total revenue goal for the fiscal year when the dust settled. I would have been over 100% with OV Group and *even higher* if she hadn't handed my largest consuming customer to the government team.

"It was also 14% year-over-year growth for the territory – 2nd best on the team. Others with that improvement exceeded revenue goal, but I did not. I guess that's neither here nor there – my goals were just set higher. The average territory needed to do about 12% growth year-over-year.

"I felt pretty good about the turnaround in the market since the territory hit 85% the year prior under my predecessor. It was a win in my book – even though I technically did not hit goal after all of those roadblocks. Most people in the division didn't hit goal, but that wasn't really a lot of solace. Oh, well - it was over and I needed to move forward and be better. Take my learnings and apply them going forward. There were plenty of lessons to go around.

"It's a fast and furious June," Vincent recalled. "Then it's like everybody breathes a sigh of relief until after 4th of July. You find out about all of the massive changes. And then it's off to the races again. Some people take vacations then. You go on a bunch of company trips and team offsites – you're practically traveling all of July and August. And then they wonder in September why few people have any new pipeline."

I recognized the buildings and could tell we were getting close to the Minneapolis Majestech-Ware office now owned by CTMI.

We drove past the 365 Nicollet Apartments, The Grand Hotel, several very large office buildings and the Target Center. At each stop, pedestrians scrambled about their morning business. The sky was currently relatively bleak. It was typical of the preponderance of my Minnesota experiences.

"I had my year-end review. Considering Miranda did my first quarterly review and my 2 subsequent ones with Quintana were excellent, I was expecting a solid raise, bonus and stock allocation. Instead, she absolutely ripped me to shreds. Humiliated me. Shocked me."

He stopped there. I was surprised. Nobody ripped Vincent to shreds. Even the old Keith Dickhauser appraisals that called him out for lacking polish and being difficult to control praised him for being the best driver of results he'd ever met. And this was a young, 20-something Vincent Scott. From everything this version was relaying to me, Vincent now kept his head down, was humble and played the game – be it with Luther Perry in his previous role when his leaders changed rules multiple times in an attempt to unseat him from the #1 position to Quintana's continued attacks on his character and chances of success.

"It was completely out of nowhere," he continued. "Not to mention, she was on her way out. She hated Minneapolis and she got her buddy Floyd Irving to move her to the Large Business Group working for him. She moved back to Mexico.

"She could have given me a fair shake, specifically since the only thing separating me from my last perfect quarterly appraisal she gave me and this moment was me taking a truncated paternity leave and coming back early to have the best year the territory had had in 5 years. I should have stayed out for the full 3 months.

"Instead, I got zero bonus. No stock rewards. A black mark on my record. Heck, Miranda had given me $10K for a *quarter* working for her the year prior. I got no raise and no stock and she wrote on my appraisal that I obtained 'insufficient results.' It was the kiss of death. She stopped short of checking the box that I was to go on a performance plan – because she knew she couldn't possibly justify it, but for all practical purposes I was marked as damaged goods and all but on my way out of the company."

"I can't believe it," I commented with shock. "How could she get away with it? Why in the world would she do that?"

"It gets worse," he replied. "We solicit for feedback from peers via a link we elect to send from our profile. We select who it goes to, but we don't see the feedback. Of course, I sent it to a handful of colleagues and teammates who I worked with often and I know for a fact gave me rave reviews. They even forwarded them to me! And Quintana did not include any of those positive comments in my appraisal as would be customary.

"She *proactively* found someone to comment on one time she claimed I did not follow up on an e-mail, when it was a vendor's responsibility – not mine. She included that situation where someone dropped the ball ordering meals for an event and because it was my customer, she blamed me."

"Surely, you fought it," I interjected.

"I don't have a lot of fight left for that sort of thing," Vincent replied, the weariness evident in his voice. "At the urging of others, I finally wrote a several page response to my appraisal that she legally had to include with it, calling out all of the discrepancies and my direct response to each false statement she made.

"Additionally, she cited in my appraisal that I needed serious work on my CTMI value story, pitch and data transformation story when meeting with customers. Of course, in my rebuttal, I also called attention to the fact she visited a whopping 1 client with me *while living in Minneapolis* and shunning numerous requests to join me in customer meetings, and after the one meeting she did go to, she praised me at all of those things. It was utterly disgusting. She had no shame.

"News of my status made the rounds in senior leadership, and the perception of me was what Quintana said – that I wasn't a fit for my role. Miranda even called me, having heard about what happened from her many former colleagues. She obviously knew the truth, and basically told me I had no choice but to go to HR. That was the last thing I wanted to do."

"Why's that?"

"Because I knew from experience it would achieve absolutely nothing. Heck, that was the whole thing at the root of what happened at ABM – my team reported Keith Dickhauser's illegal activity and I stood with them, we were promised he'd be dealt with, he wasn't, I expressed to HR I feared the retaliation that was coming and he retaliated anyway. Against *only me*. It led to an expensive, excruciating 3-year court pursuit. HR did nothing but stand in my way and keep me down, aiding the company.

"Would CTMI be any different? I didn't have faith that they would be. But I agreed to report Quintana to HR because yes, this situation was completely unfair. I followed Miranda's advice despite my hunches.

"In the end, I wasted hours upon hours having to recount every story I have already told you today. They forced me to live and die by *just one* reason Quintana targeted me that fell under an HR violation. Let's be real – there were several. Several that fall into every facet of HR but others as well.

"And, in the end, HR did *literally nothing* – claiming the one I chose was not the reason she targeted me and picked one of the litany of examples I gave them of her harassment that didn't fit that one bucket. Of course, it wasn't the only one; they cited *one* reason why *that* category didn't fit everything I gave them, and dropped it. It left me very disenfranchised with a black mark on my record and one foot out the door.

"At the beginning of that process, I actually had to meet with Quintana to cover my concerns with my appraisal. She refused to let me speak from my notes because she wouldn't let me open my laptop. She would not let me finish a sentence – she interrupted me over and over again. Heck, she only gave me 30 minutes and showed up 5 minutes late after I had prepped for *hours* just for this conversation.

"She told me point blank I was wasting my time building a case; that sometimes I can just be a machine and I need to do more to build personal relationships. Calling me a machine was actually one of the best compliments she ever gave me - I quite enjoyed it. Anyhow, the conversation with her went nowhere so I had to submit the escalation to HR. And HR took *months* to ultimately do absolutely nothing.

50

"I got a new boss starting in July – Jeremy Rivers. He was an up-and-comer. He had been a seller, territory manager and was now a Director. Everybody loved him and spoke highly of him. Super charismatic, knowledgeable – a guy who controlled the room. He was a star. And now he's inherited me thinking I am a problem child, waste of space who should be ushered out the door. It was discouraging and disheartening. ABG looked better and better."

"What about the other internal jobs?" I asked.

"They disappeared. They took Renee's Large Business Group team and broke it up into industry verticals and that job vanished. The Hardware Specialist role was realigned to another market. I had to stay the course branded a loser or put my tails between my legs and leave for a relatively small vendor.

"It was such a slap in the face, especially after I came back 6 weeks early from paternity leave to close all of those deals and I got every freaking pain-in-the-butt one of them!" Vincent's frustration was evident.

"I mean, there was so much back and forth on some of these deals. Piper Airport had such a discombobulated procurement process and the people we were working with contradicted each other constantly. So much waffling on that deal and I finally got it done but for a fraction of what I was led to believe it would be from the partner. Of course, that puts egg on my face.

"Then there was Anson Marketing – the one that badmouthed me in my absence to try to strong-arm CTMI into dropping their pants on the deal. I wound up going over that nasty CIO's head to the CEO and CFO and got the deal done; of course, they were going to use our product for another of CTMI's major clients and that client's account team stole my deal. *Every* deal has a long and twisted story. So, there was yet another deal that transpired for a fraction of what it should have been. Another hit.

"I learned a ton – mostly from the lost deals or the ones where I got put through the wringer by internal process. Furthermore, I realized ABG did me no favors – I introduced them into so many accounts and they yielded next to nothing while Mick Logan and Merit Productivity turned what deals I handed them into gold.

"I entered the new fiscal year, starting July 2017, with a completely new outlook. I realized the vendors were overwhelmingly lousy, but Mick would aggressively chase business. I'd give him everything I could. And I realized because of how hard it was to get these deals done that I needed a ton more pipeline to cover quota; these vendors weren't doing it so I had to do it myself.

"Finally, chasing all of these start-up's and small unmanaged businesses made some gains, but they didn't offset the lack of new business in the already managed accounts. I had counted on the vendors to drive that after I prospected the pipeline; they failed. So, having kept these new logos I signed and working to grow them, I would turn my focus on the other managed accounts, drive my own pipeline and hand everything to Mick."

"I'm astounded," I commented, as we approached the CTMI building and Vincent pulled into the employee garage. "Most people would have taken that experience and crumbled. Or at least just gone through the motions feeling defeated."

"That was never an option," Vincent replied. "I had something all new to prove."

Chapter 4 – The Path Forward

Vincent parked his Aston Martin on the second level of the garage, away from most of the cars already parked. He put the top back on the convertible. We exited and walked toward the staircase as he clicked on the security alarm.

"I won't be too long," he commented. "There's a coffee shop on the first floor. Good Wi-Fi. You'll be OK?"

"Yes, absolutely," I responded. "I can get caught up on e-mail."

"Perfect. See you shortly."

He took the elevator and I kept walking, into the coffee shop area where I grabbed a skinny mocha. I checked e-mail and checked in with the wife and my mind wandered to the discussion of the morning.

What I found the most fascinating is the human element of the man. All I saw, outside of a few substantial conversations over the last decade, was the successes – the promotions, the social posts, his writing. He seemed to have reached a level of acceptance as to what part the ABM saga had played in his life, but no job he did there or since had been without its own unique debilitating challenges. Was this truly the fate of a supernova talent like Vincent Scott – literally constant barriers and setbacks, even one of which would cripple the normal person?

It interested me most that he said he did not have as much fight as he once did.

Roughly an hour passed. The coffee was good; not the best of its ilk I had enjoyed, but serviceable.

Vincent approached my table. He did not appear to show his cards as to whether or not the meeting he had just come from went well. He, too, grabbed a coffee and joined me at the table.

"How'd that go?" I asked.

"I'd say it took a turn for the interesting, but I suppose I'll know soon enough," he commented. "So - where were we?"

Here he goes again, shifting gears on me. I figured I would follow along.

"You had the best year the territory had had in 5 years and were thanked with a horrible appraisal after 3 perfect ones and the only thing between appraisal 3 and appraisal 4 was you coming back early from paternity leave to close all 11 deals you needed. Then Quintana went back to Mexico. That about it?"

"Yeah. You make it sound brutal," Vincent said, managing a smile.

"I have to ask – do you still think about that time often? Or other times in your career? What lasting impressions has your career had on you?"

Vincent did not ponder this question long. "I have a lot of fond memories and then I have baggage I certainly carry. Years of counseling have taught me that I never feel like I'm good enough, which is why I'm a perfectionist and why I drive myself beyond normal limits. So, I certainly remember the times in my career when I most felt inadequate – namely when ABM fired me and when Quintana inexplicably tried to destroy me. It did not help when Wireless Horizons replaced me to save money and I got laid off or when Tel-Cell refused to promote me after I saved the market.

"But I also have a lot of fond memories. Starting that ABM division from scratch cold calling off spreadsheets and making stick tallies for call counts, lugging around physical directories of the territories we called. The growth that division had – interviewing a thousand people, making daily sales speeches and deciding what would feed into our eventual auto-dialer. Writing synopses of each market we were calling. Manipulating the campaigns and leads and tracking the stats. I was a junkie of the numbers."

He stopped, which made me wonder if there were other positive elements he recalled.

"Any other fond memories?"

"Mostly just people. When I was first promoted at ABM, I had some stellar and fun sales teams. When Jeff Mason and Ted Benton and those folks worked for me in the call center, and we'd make jokes and laugh and listen to music.

"Everything since ABM has been less rewarding; it's been me chasing where I thought I once was or could have been or where I thought I should be."

"Have you gotten there?"

"In some ways, yes," Vincent said thoughtfully. "Financially, no question. I miss what I did then. But I had to come to realize that it could never be recreated and because of the horribly toxic work environment I was ready to go anyway.

Heck, I was supposed to interview for my fourth promotion the day after I got fired. And running into Keith Dickhauser *yet again* really put it all into perspective."

"Again?" I asked. "In addition to seeing him at the restaurant?"

"Oh, yes. But we'll get there. I think what sticks with me most, sadly, is the times where I unjustly lost what I had or where I was unfairly targeted or when my best was *the* best but still not good enough. But that hasn't been all bad. It has fueled me. And I can tell you that I was never more motivated than after what Quintana did to me."

"Really?" I raved. "OK - tell me about that."

"Well, I had just been awarded a stigma – I was going to a rockstar new boss who undoubtedly now thought I was a waste of space. Part of me was upset with the unfair perspective of me that existed. However, there's something to be said for people having zero expectation of you or having written you off – it's easier to impress them.

"I realized quickly I needed to do a couple of things. One – level set with my new boss Jeremy and ensure he knew I vehemently disagreed with everything Quintana stood for and had done; let him know I was not a believer at all in going to HR but numerous trusted advisors had convinced me I really had no choice based on the circumstances. Second - I had to put my money where my mouth was. I had to shine. I had to make a comeback of epic proportion."

"Unbelievable to hear that you felt you had to make a 'comeback' - specifically after such a good year."

"It wasn't just that. Many of the customers, certainly my team, most of the vendors – they were all ecstatic to have me. I was constructing newsletters and events and webinars for these customers - it was the most contact they had ever gotten. The team was getting coaching and direction, patience and leadership. And the vendors were being proactively led into pipeline instead of the other way around.

"The missing piece for me with vendors is I had to take the bull by the horns – directing that activity. I had to motivate them with the only things they really cared about – new services business – the deployment of our solutions. I had to find the way to entice them with potential for the high margin stuff they did while getting them to do what I wanted them to do in the interim. And I rallied solely behind

Mick and Merit Productivity because they were the only ones getting anything done for me at the time.

"This was a ruthless business. I couldn't be friends with anyone. All the friendly banter I had with everyone hadn't amounted to a hill of beans when I got obliterated on my appraisal and branded as washed-up garbage. I had to selfishly manage my business and my time. I had to play probability and odds, betting on people and vendors who would actually get things done. I had to rally behind large deals and scale with the team and the vendors on the smaller ones, all under my watchful eye and dispassionate temperament.

"I canceled most all cadence calls I previously had with the vendors. They were pointless. They turned into us sitting around for 30 minutes talking about nothing, with the vendors asking me to help them do their job. No thanks.

"I spent hours in the early-going putting together a relatively robust spreadsheet with every account in the patch, account details, contacts, what they owned and highlighted what could be sold to them. I stack-ranked them by priority, propensity and potential. It was an idea I stole from my new teammate, Johnny Smythe. And it was brilliant, because I wound up referencing it every single day – sometimes multiple times.

"The first half of my year would be spent prospecting and driving pipeline. The back half would be singularly focused on closing down absolutely everything compiled in the first half.

"I spent a ton of time on LinkedIn trying to connect with everyone who was Director or above at the accounts in the territory – I got over 500 new contacts within a couple of weeks. I authored a survey based specifically on the types of conversations most customers wanted to have that could lead to opportunities – related to how they could utilize data, better collaboration and some of the applications they used today and how ours could complement them. Using the prospecting and surveys, I drove 16 C-Suite conversations within the accounts in July alone. It was unprecedented. Never been done.

"I was reporting all of my activity and results to Jeremy, who seemed extremely receptive. He came across as very willing to give me a 'clean slate' and expressed optimism, but I've grown so skeptical over the years I never knew if he meant it or was just saying it. But it didn't matter. I was going to give it everything I had.

"And what I was doing was working. It was getting conversations and driving pipeline. Within the first quarter of the new fiscal year, I had at least 5 times the pipeline of anyone else doing my role in the United States – in the way of total opportunities and potential revenue. My survey was shared company-wide as a best practice. I won an award for it.

"But driving conversations and pipeline didn't mean anything unless it led to results. Quintana had put it out there that I wasn't a closer and wasn't capable of leading the team. So, I had only just begun. I had to deliver results.

"Her betrayal was also motivating in other areas – I kicked it up a notch on my gym workouts. I love doing the weekly step challenges on my fitness band and at the time I would win every week at all costs. My biggest rival then was my old friend Jeff Mason!"

"From ABM?" I asked, smiling.

"Yes," Vincent responded. "One and the same. Through the years, he and a handful of others have remained close friends. In fact, that quarter for our team kickoff I was in Dallas and got to see a Rangers game with him and hang out a bit. We still watch and quote *Cocktail* every chance we get."

"That movie is a classic!" I concurred.

"For me, exercising – especially at 4 or 5 in the morning – gets me going, but it's the almost mechanical exertion of the body that takes my mind off everything else. It gives me energy. And it's one of the very, very few things I can control. From there, in my day, everything else can and will unravel. But those opening hours when I'm strengthening and driving myself harder and freeing my mind – I'm in complete control as long as my body can take it.

"At work, I often can control very little. So, of course, I control what I can from a probability perspective. I can control how much outreach I do and how many people I try to connect with. If the average seller reaches out to 1 or 2 people trying to get a C-Suite meeting and I reach out to 30 to 50, who has the better chance? I may not get in with the CEO or CIO or CFO on the first shot, but I can certainly meet with their VP's or a COO or someone who can help me get in that door. It gets me at the pulse of the organization to understand the landscape and challenges. And every bit of that I can use to further the cause out there.

"Now, I'm also keeping that contact on my newsletter touches and marketing touches and inviting them to events. It may be a month or a year later, but we'll talk again. And if you replicate that effort at 200 accounts, you've amplified your probability of meaningful connections and contacts.

"Furthermore, if I get a meeting, I will walk out with pipeline. Sometimes 5 or 6 different types of opportunities based on where the conversation goes. And from there, I plug in the technical specialists who handle those workloads and let them run. I nudge and prod and ensure the ball keeps moving down the field.

"Lucy Burke on my team actually told me once that she goes down her list of accounts every single day, asking herself what – if anything – she can do to impact any opportunity at that account. If there's something that can or needs to be done, like a note to the customer or a vendor or something internal that needs to happen, she does it. If not, she moves on. Down the list, every single day. And I don't care if you have 10 accounts or 200, it works. I adopted that practice that summer of 2017 and it worked like a charm – I left no stone unturned every day.

"Deal cycles and milestones are all over the place. Where I got buried the year prior, not to mention having zero support from my boss, was drowning in not only the activities that needed to happen but the internal baloney and blockers and noise. It wasn't enough to find a deal and try to craft it; there were internal bodies you had to go through to get anything approved or approve incentives or to help you put together collateral or reports. And they had to be aggressively managed just like everything else.

"I had to learn to and how to best get them to do what I wanted when I wanted. And what worked best – everywhere – was humility. Coming to them, hat in hand, graciously asking for feedback or guidance or coaching or their expertise – even if that was the farthest thing from what I really needed. Gently, calmly inquiring about status, being understanding of what was also their undoubtedly overwhelming schedule. Getting flies with honey.

"Even when... no, *especially when* I was just trying to get what I wanted, I was the exact opposite of what I was in my 20's. I knew what I wanted and how things needed to go, but I'd manhandle the situation or even just tell them how to do their job when they pushed back. It was not the way to gain their advocacy and assistance. Even if they were completely incompetent, I had to coax them to deliver what I needed. I learned to tell a story. To paint a picture. And I learned how to get these internal CTMI resources to provide whatever I needed to get the deal done.

"It felt like – with Jeremy, and with the new team I was on, that there was a different comradery. Charlotte Baines had had a really good year and got promoted. Lucy Burke left for a lateral move for an industry vertical, after they split up the Large Business Group. Stu Sanders left to go work for Charlotte. I was now on a team with guys like Johnny Smythe, Will Matthews – guys that had been around for 5-6 years and knew the ropes. They had experienced good years and so-so years, but they were grounded and they were real. They were fun to talk to. They were family men with kids and they were a bit older than I was.

"I've always succeeded by finding out what good sellers do and assimilating as much of it as I could into my process, then trying to do it better. Combining best practices and hustle has gotten me this far in multiple industries I knew relatively nothing about.

"Johnny Smythe showed me what he called his 'bible': a spreadsheet of every account in the territory and all of the vital statistics – key dates, vendors attached to the account, and what they owned; he'd highlight certain things, outline what his opportunity was at each account, and he would reference this spreadsheet constantly. It was time-consuming, but it was something I could do and that I saw value in. So I replicated it.

"I took it further, aligning with specific vendors for sales plays on certain topics. Then I would find vendors that specialized in certain types of sales plays – be it analytics programs, security, collaboration tools, etc. Not only would I have them create collateral I could share strategically, but we'd do webinars and events together. A 1:Many philosophy designed solely to get 1:1 meetings. Again, law of averages. And if you do enough of that with 200 accounts, you're bound to get a dozen or so conversations with every play you run.

"The first fiscal quarter of the new year, I had the most pipeline in the company. By far.

"I had a new boss's boss, too – her name was Janet Leary. She was great – energetic, positive. A complete 180 from what I was reporting into before which was all doom and gloom. She also told me she bought my book."

Vincent laughed. I could sense very much that the period of time he was describing was a night and day difference from the ordeal he had just outlined. But then he got a bit morose again.

"I couldn't shake this feeling of inadequacy. I just assumed everyone I encountered thought I was trash. But at times, it also fueled me. My completely unqualified miserable excuse of a manager had awakened in me a fire I had never encountered. I had never had to prove myself like this before. And I was bent on giving it absolutely everything I had.

"Jake Zuniga dubbed me 'Man on Fire.' Yes – like the Denzel Washington movie. And I was. I had taken matters into my own hands and the bull by the horns – doing my own prospecting, outreach, meetings, driving my own pipeline and then picking whatever vendor – typically Mick Logan at Merit Productivity – to run with it.

"I was not at the mercy of anyone's weekly cadences – I dictated who I talked to and when. Vendors had to earn my time by actually doing something, and I held customers accountable to the milestones they agreed upon. I raised the flag every time there was so much as a sniff of a compete scenario or situation where we could benefit from extra internal help and then I managed those resources, too. If they were going to get credit for my wins, by goodness I was going to get their efforts."

"I love it," I replied. "And, let me guess – you blew your numbers out of the water."

He shook his head. "Unfortunately, it doesn't really work like that because the sales cycles are all over the place. But we were getting pipeline in droves and some of it was bound to close. We were driving deals forward and I had more in play than anyone else. Yes – law of averages dictated that it would pan out. It just couldn't come soon enough for a guy who felt like he was racing against time.

"It was around that time Abby quit working at the hospital and stayed home with Sydney, so the pressure was really on. I never anticipated I'd be supporting a family by myself. Elizabeth turned 10 and was back into volleyball season. I was drastically burning the candle on both ends. Jake thought sure I'd burn out. But I said and felt that was impossible.

"I differed from many others in my role because I didn't care about or know about the technology behind the solutions. But I didn't need to, because I could get in more C-Suite rooms than anyone else and bring the smart guys with me. It had taken me a year and a half, but I had mastered the process. Now I just had to drum up the deals and close them down.

"Remember - this territory had never really done well before me. Years ago, a predecessor of mine had audited everyone in town who was an existing customer and squeezed out enough additional revenue to hit goal before he departed the company. He destroyed his number but also infuriated a lot of folks.

"I'd come to find out that a lot of the people who wouldn't talk to me of the 200 accounts I oversaw were sour at us because of just that very thing. They felt CTMI and Majestech-Ware had only shown up when we wanted to sell them something. There was no relationship; no partnership. It took my team and I being communicative and consistent to change that tide.

"As time went by, more and more 'new' relationships sprung up – and they would come from everywhere. It might be a new contact who downloaded a virtual brochure about one of our products – and I'd reach out to them myself *and* add them to our newsletter and webinar lists, connect with them on social media and follow their posts. People would show up on these webinars or at events I sponsored that had never returned an e-mail or call, but now we were shaking hands and there was a personal connection.

"In hindsight, it's funny to look back on these folks knowing where those deals did or didn't go.

"The most interesting deal that popped up was Trucking Group International," Vincent continued.

"Yeah, I know them – but they're not in Minneapolis are they? They're kind of big..."

Vincent chuckled. "Sometimes our account groupings don't make a lot of sense. Right – they are headquartered in Los Angeles, but their largest dealer, who buys all of the services for the parent company, is in Minneapolis. And if our Large Business Group accounts don't buy enough or are forecasted to not hit quota, they will dump them on us. We're like the minor leagues – always looking for prospects and getting the ones who didn't pan out."

"Quite an interesting position," I commented.

"Yeah, it can be thankless sometimes. But that's why it pays to know how to move the numbers around and to have 200 accounts. It can be easier to find a diamond in the rough or two, and then you blow it out."

"Funny how sales works like that," I said.

"You have to understand the inner workings of the game. It's like 9-Ball. Being good, knowing the angles and making your shots matter, but luck and knowing the art plays a part.

"So, for this new fiscal year I had been assigned TGI. They wouldn't give me the time of day. They had recently changed CEO and CIO and when that happened, all of the potential deals on the table at any of their dealers died. They wiped the slate clean. The new CIO – Mike Jericho – notoriously hated vendors of any kind. He wouldn't return my calls; I managed to get one of his project managers to talk to me but that never really went anywhere meaningful. I knew I had to do something different.

"So, I went over and around his head – anywhere I could think to go."

"I like it," I exclaimed. "How did that go over?"

"Well... it certainly worked. I managed to connect with the new CEO, the CFO and the Treasurer of the Board. But it royally ticked off the CIO."

"Oh boy," I remarked. "Do tell."

"It was actually somewhat innocent. I found a guy internally at Majestech-Ware whose wife worked for one of the TGI dealers in Los Angeles by playing around on LinkedIn. Turns out, she knew all kinds of insider information. She shared it with him and he shared it with me.

"Feels kind of like *Wall Street*." I smirked. He laughed.

"Greed is good," he replied. "Anyhow, I used LinkedIn to meet the other C-Suites and this guy in L.A. actually got permission from his boss to help me on the deal even though it wasn't in his jurisdiction. It was great for the company, of course – I mean, imagine selling our data platform to a trucking company with hundreds of agents. Because we got in front of everyone above the CIO, they forced him to take a meeting with me."

"Holy cow," I said. "How awkward was that?"

"Definitely awkward. But I see myself like Batman sometimes – I'm the hero that can be the villain."

I rewarded him with more laughter.

He continued, "Look - what's the worst thing that happens? He hates my guts and talks trash about me to his team, but I inch closer to a deal? I don't have to be liked or loved – I'm paid to be an evangelist of my business and my customers and my people. It's a numbers' game. I know I can't win them all but I'm happy to go down swinging."

"So, I take it that it went well after he met with you?"

"Not at all," Vincent replied quickly. "It went horribly, actually.

"I did meet with Jericho. He was with a couple of his team members and he pretty much lambasted me and my company and all vendors the entire time – until it was just us 1:1. Then I saw a bit of a softer side, which indicated to me that he was just putting on a show for them. He was actually honest and transparent when we talked. And I noticed this was a pattern through our entire relationship: he was cold and callous in e-mail and on calls and in meetings with others present. But when it was just us, he was cordial. Almost likeable. *Almost.*"

"Wow - so what ended up happening?"

"He went dark on me for a bit. Their biggest international problem was lack of ability to communicate amongst the dealers. To share data. To share, frankly, mission critical information about shipments with one another when multiple dealers had to get involved. And our solution would have fixed all that. And they knew it. But they were very stubborn.

"He was determined to figure out their own way of doing it. He was a new CIO and needed a win. They had spent millions upon millions of dollars creating a spinoff branch just for innovation – and it had tanked. It was like he hated vendors so much that he refused to accept we had a better way. And our way would have been less expensive with greater ROI than any other he was researching.

"But you can change nearly anyone's mind," Vincent continued, slowing and taking a sip of his coffee. "You just have to figure out what they care about.

"Jericho had been with the company for about a year when I made a dent in his armor. He had yet to get his win. Scuttlebutt was that they were going to scrap his innovation team and give him the boot.

"I cut through the garbage and the 'sale' and just asked him how I could help him win. What would it look like. What mattered.

"Profit margins were excruciatingly low. They had lost a couple of major shipping contracts. Their 600 dealers worldwide were using about 200 different systems for what ours would do and the most-used system was used differently everywhere it was in place.

"Because of the inconsistency and the low margins, they were really unattractive to potential new trucking companies they tried to sign into their consortium. Jericho had a vision of creating a platform whereby he could resell solutions and services to all of these potential new dealers – not just IT, but intranet, websites, ecommerce. Really anything revenue generating. Staplers and pens, even. 'You sign up with TGI, and you get this value-added service,' basically.

"One thing I've learned over the years is everyone has to leave the bargaining table happy when you make a deal. There's a little bit of give and a whole lot of get on each side."

"The 'holy sales trinity'!" I exclaimed.

"You remembered," Vincent said, beaming. "Yes. The customer, the company, and you. The customer has to gain value, an answer to a problem, a return on investment, increased margin, prestige, and to look like a hero to their boss or shareholders. The company – *your* company – has to address a key metric or more, make money, realize profit, add a logo, win a fan, etch out higher market penetration. And you. *You* have to win something in the deal, too, or what the heck are we fighting for?

"Some sellers screw it all up. They bend over backwards to get a customer to sign for any amount and they miss goal and their company doesn't make money. Or they only care about how they get paid, and they undercut the customer who turns sour and may not renew and may give negative press.

"All that matters is that everyone gets a win. So that's what I did with TGI.

"I worked with our app development team. I brought in our partner development team. I even found another vendor who built solutions on top of our software specifically for the trucking and logistics industry.

"The other thing is internal politics – you've got to raise the flag. You've got to get people in the boat with you – as many as possible. You've got to be careful not to cause a commotion when there's no real deal and you also often have to keep everyone on task yourself. But if you have a potential deal or a potential loss, it's important people who can help you know about it. Never go down alone.

"I brought in the division GM of our analytics business, for crying out loud. She flew to L.A. with me and a half-dozen others I engaged on this opportunity. We put on a dog and pony show to end all dog and pony shows. And we had the CEO, CFO, CIO and his CTO in the room."

"Unbelievable! And you closed it down!" I belted out, certain that Vincent's hard work was going to pay off at this point in the story.

Vincent shook his head. "No. No, we didn't. Because no matter what I did for Jericho, he was just a bitter guy who had to do it himself. He made fun of me in the meeting, saying in front of his boss that I forced myself on them and basically put him in the position of having to tell me 'no' twice because I had involved his CEO. He tried to bring up the amount of time he had waited for answers while I was going back and forth internally to try to basically create a program for him that had not existed previously and translated that to my inefficiency. His CTO rudely pointed out every negative thing he could about our organization along with how he could do what we were proposing better than we could."

"You've got to be kidding me! How ungrateful. I guess you cut bait?"

"Absolutely not. I can understand egomaniacs. Sure, on paper it looked like I had just wasted the time of a lot of nice people who had flown in from around the world. I know Jericho expected me to put my tail between my legs. And I always like to do the opposite of what people expect. Kind of like when Quintana pushed me one foot out the door. I thrust myself fully back in the business with both feet.

"I knew Mike Jericho would never consciously sign a deal with CTMI or Majestech-Ware – he had too much pride. But come to find out, Darren Miller – the Managing Partner at Accord Business Group – also knew Jericho. They had worked together years ago.

"ABG was one of our vendors, with the ability to re-sell the licensing for our stuff indirectly. I went to Darren, sold him on the idea of re-selling this framework to TGI, and I'd back off completely. Jericho would never have to hear from me again. I would hand the deal to Nick Aragon, who would manage the account for ABG and Darren Miller would ice the deal with Mike Jericho. They went to lunch one day and it was full steam ahead.

"It *worked?*"

"Sometimes, we are the only thing standing in our own way to a deal or a goal. I knew this guy hated me, and he had every right to – I wouldn't take no for an answer and I went over his head to get what I wanted. Sure, he was a jerk, but I forced myself to the table. I had taken it as far as I could, but I realized I'd need help to get it across the finish line. Someone else had to win. I guess it had to become a sales square as opposed to a trinity.

"I have learned to take my ego out of the equation."

"What's it feel like to say that?" I asked Vincent. Knowing him for a decade, this was quite the revelation.

"I've gained and won far more by helping others win. I'd give anything to go back to my ABM days with the mindset I have now. Of course, I wouldn't feel this way had I not gone out the way I did and had to fight to get back.

"I entered Majestech-Ware content to just be a contributor at best. I didn't know the technology, I desperately needed a job after the Joe Downey management consultant firm ripped me off, and I was completely overwhelmed by the products and systems and processes of this company. I'd fill a seat, play a role and hopefully survive. But then, I somehow became the best.

"Then I got humbled again – humiliated by Quintana. But something new happened in all of that – I was no longer just fueled by my only child syndrome and plight for ABM redemption or to make my parents proud of me. Now it was to prove Quintana Navarro wrong. It was to show these people that she was gravely mistaken; that I wasn't a waste of space or just Miranda Bond's boy. That I hadn't already peaked.

"So, finding everyone I could to get in the boat and be on the sales team for these opportunities was what I was going to do. My strength was driving the relationships and pipeline, so I'd thrive on that and then hand off deals to other people. They loved me for it. No one else was driving this type of activity for them.

"Then, it was my old management skills – making sure to lead the team, communicate often and thoroughly, set milestones and drive toward them, hold accountable. And I did and do everything I can to point out what people are doing right. Making ideas theirs, not mine. The old me had to be the smartest guy in the room. Now, I am quite content with being the dumbest."

I shook my head, "That's the *smartest* thing I've ever heard you say."

"People want to feel good. They want to feel valued. And if I'm hogging all the credit, there's limited room for that. Sure, the old me was great at artificially pumping people up and selling them on selling a product that barely worked. I was selling an image. Selling money-making. Now, I'm selling involvement. Engagement. Making a difference. And it's more honorable and lucrative than anything I've ever done."

66

"Is it fulfilling?"

Vincent stopped. He did not answer right away.

"Fulfilling," he repeated slowly, taking in the word and clearly contemplating his reply. "Ask me again sometime."

We continued our coffee and were about halfway complete.

"What else is on the agenda for today?" I asked.

"I figured I'd give you a tour of my office," Vincent replied. "And then, if you're up for it, I've got a little surprise."

"Sounds good – I'll take whatever I can get of your time today."

"You got it."

"Let's change the subject for a bit. Care if I ask some philosophy and style questions?"

"Fire away."

Chapter 5 – The Salesman's Two Cents

"How would you describe yourself as a seller, and how you got your start?"

"I'm just a guy who is passionate about selling and came across it by happenstance. I thought I was getting myself into a customer service role after college. Turned out it was a pretty intense selling gig. Within a month, I was tops in the office and very quickly rose through the ranks. Over the years, I was fortunate to be promoted and in different industries and functions. I've worked in telecom and advertising and now in technology. It's had its highs and lows; triumphs and heartbreaks. It's been incredible overall. A very rewarding experience and I continue to learn every day. I'd consider myself a student of sales."

"What's the best thing about working in sales?" I asked.

"That you'll always have more story to tell. More people to meet. More challenges to take on. If you're passionate about selling, there will always be a home for you."

"What key concepts would you say you hold most dear?"

"That's a great question. I think we're all connected in the sales ecosystem, whether it's working with a customer, with a partner, or training or managing someone. All of those relationships require understanding of the person on the other end, what their motivations are, and how to best add value for them. It's so important to focus on having a positive interaction and relationship with everybody that you're touching in the sales food chain.

"You also know I love the holy sales trinity; the customer, the company, and you. Those three entities have to benefit from every deal that's constructed. If somebody loses in that deal, it's a bad deal. Walk away from it. Don't do it.

"It's also about people and process. If you've got the right people – people that have the right approach, work ethic, endurance – doing the right process – the one that's got the highest probability at success each leg of the selling process, you're going to achieve success. Period. That simple.

"It's important to have an over-arching strategy to encompass every facet of your selling process – from planning, prospecting and outreach to continued touches, meetings, optimization of resources, management of pipeline and bringing deals to closure, and post-sales.

"At each step or leg of the process of selling, we must be focused on that step and not looking too far ahead into the steps to come. When I'm prospecting, I can't focus on the end result – I have to sell the connection. Then the meeting. Then the relationship. Certainly, we think about potential outcomes, but we cannot look too much into steps we haven't gotten to yet. It's like looking to next Sunday's football game before playing this one."

"What's the most important component or attribute of successful sales?"

Vincent laughed. "Now, there's a question. If you had asked me that 10 years ago, I would have probably said work ethic or tenacity. Maybe passion and personality. I thought hard work trumped all. But at this point, I'd say endurance.

"There are so many times we'll be told no, where relationships or deals go heinously awry even in the eleventh hour of deal-making, where internal politics, bureaucracy, or process impedes us instead of helps. The way that we react and respond to those setbacks determine our destiny and our durability in this game. And the amount of those setbacks we can take in stride while keeping a steady hand on the wheel will ensure better outcomes.

"Years ago, I had a VP at ABM Advertising – Cesar Fiorintino – who wrote on my appraisal that I was a supernova but lacked polish. I had no idea what he meant. I thought I was the finished product. Looking back on that late 20's version of me, I know now exactly what he meant. Discipline. An ability to choose my battles and gain consensus and listen to others. Truly listen. And to not react hastily to everything that doesn't go the way I think it should.

"If we react poorly, if we get frustrated and complain, that's not only going to create a negative brand for ourselves, but it's also going to ensure we won't reach our potential."

"How do you do it? How do you persist and maintain positivity in the face of setbacks?"

"Put one foot in front of the other. At all costs. I take solace in my routines. We all know what needs to be done; we just have to *do it*.

"I mean it when I say I had a brutal year working with Quintana. I learned a ton, but it was pretty much all on my own. I lost a lot of deals – some fairly, and some unfairly. But I never would have been prepared for deals I've won since had it not been for that trial by fire.

"And on the days I'm 'not feeling it' I'm still up at 4 or 4:30 and in the gym so my head's right. Then I consume massive amounts of coffee. And I prioritize my day. I have non-negotiables every day that have to get done no matter what else may come my way.

"You can't optimize your day unless you unclutter your day; if there is something that's scheduled for that day that isn't paramount to your process and you've got other things that take priority, offer to move that meeting and push it out to a time where it's more conducive and really prioritize what you've got to get done that day. Schedule everything. Even time to maybe take a lunch or read a book or do your training or prospecting or even drive time – doing so cuts down on needless stress and being over-booked.

"When in doubt, I fall back on process. Sure, I tweak and evolve process, but process has never failed me."

"What sets you apart from other sellers?"

"For me, it's all about relationships and knowing the playing field and tools at my disposal and how to use them. That's it. There's a lot of tools that are out there that can help you find your target audience and learn about them and get in the room. Nothing will ever replace the face-to-face, though. And, once you're there, you have to keep earning your place in the room with the customer by bringing unique value.

"I'm communicative. Sometimes overly so. Being transparent and informing folks of everything I'm doing to build a community around my efforts. Passive sales stuff – staying top of mind. Plus, being super responsive. Even if you don't know the answer, even if you don't know the answer right away, even if you've got to pull in additional resources, as long as folks see that you're responding and you're active on their request, it will further the relationship.

"A lot of times clients will do business because of that fact. I've had many people tell me over the years that they have done business with me because I responded, and I got them the answers that they needed. They knew I was working on it. Even if I didn't have the answer right away, I'd send regular updates. They will pay more for that level of service. It's a true partnership.

"Think about it, it takes just a couple of seconds to just send a quick note to a client letting them know that they're top of mind and that you're working on it. I think it comes back to prioritization. Sure, there are a lot of functions in my job.

There's a lot of functions in my side hustle where I spend a lot of time blogging or speaking. I'm also a husband and dad of two kids. There's a lot of blessings in my life, and it all comes down to priorities, but making sure that you're responsive and in tune with the needs of the folks that you're working with keeps things humming.

"You never know when that's going to come back around. It's going to benefit you. Some of these folks will move to different roles or different companies and then that's another potential prospect for you. Be very mindful of the relationship and do everything you can to devote yourself to that.

"The last thing I would highlight, talking about the perseverance piece, the relationships piece, is probability. We're in a game that can be broken down into a science and mathematics. If I'm prospecting, if I'm doing five different activities to prospect instead of one, you'd better believe I've got a better chance of getting ahold of the person that I want to reach.

"Be as opportunistic as you can but use as many mechanisms as feasible to get in front of people. Remember: upfront, you're selling a connection. Someone you can reach out to, someone who can see your posts and you can find out more about. Then, you're selling a meeting. Just a meeting. You're not selling your product or service. Figure out what you need to say to get that meeting and realize that it is a numbers game. You're going to need to try to sell a hundred meetings to get one sometimes. And that meeting isn't so you can sell – it's so you can get to know them, understand their needs, and see if there is potential for partnership between your organizations and each other. You may bring value to them neither of you could foresee. That's the idea.

"Change your messaging up, evolve, pivot, be adaptable, be coachable; You're going to alter parts of your selling process over and over through the years. Don't make drastic changes per se, but if you see a quality change that you can make, like better questions you can ask or you pick up words or best practices from a colleague, those are the types of things that are going to help your sales process get better."

"What sets you apart from other sales leaders? How do you go about leading sellers?"

"Everybody has their way of learning, being led and executing. They all have their own things that motivate them and their own reasons why they are in the game, as it were. I think before you can lead anyone, it's imperative to understand them. Just like your relationship with a potential customer or a client or with a partner or vendor, it's important to understand their motivations because ultimately that's what you're going to play to. You want to add value in any way you can to the relationship. That approach is what's going to bring results.

"When you're managing someone, it's very important to understand their drivers. Why are they there? What are their strengths? What are the components that they have recognized they want improvement on and need improvement with? A lot of times they're going to be very receptive to those areas of the business.

"The other component of that is understanding their prognosis and knowing how to diagnose a course of action. Akin to diagnosing a customer and their gaps in process, you are delivering a diagnosis to the person you're managing to address their gaps in their sales process. Not everybody is going to come to the table with every single tool in the tool bag to be a successful seller or leader. The key is to understand what they bring to the table, what areas you can work with, and what are those gaps in process.

"When you are coaching or training someone, especially from a sales vantage point, it's paramount to understand what they're innately bringing to the table in skills and personality. You must – as a leader – have or develop an ability to diagnose those gaps and prescribe modifications that will address them.

"Ultimately, you're selling change. Just like you're selling the concept of change to a customer, you're selling a salesperson on changing behaviors to yield better results. Why should they change? Why should they get rid of or jettison comfortable ways of failing or of mediocrity?

"A lot of us do what feels natural or what's most comfortable. Frankly, we may even be completely sold on why we should make a change to our process and we try it, it feels a little uncomfortable, and we regress. If we botch it a couple of times, we can go back to that comfortable way of failing. That old way worked once in a blue moon, and this new way feels bad and didn't work the two or three times I tried it, so let me go back to the old way.

"The part we're missing in that is the new way has a higher probability of success *if executed properly*. We must be willing to gamble results we know aren't our best in favor of a new, way of doing things that's clearly better, even though it is uncomfortable at first. If we successfully master this new way, our results will improve. We have to be willing to make the switch.

"Without challenge, without discomfort, there is no growth and no learning and no new experience. We can't achieve differently without a different approach.

"As leaders, we also need to understand what their desired end goal is because that's ultimately how you're going to sell change. People will change when they fear the change less than they fear the ramification of not changing. When you're leading someone, you want to make sure that they see that path. They see what they want. They've outlined their goals and what their motivations are and why they're in it so that you can continually coach them toward the change that will better them.

"As coaches and leaders, we help them construct those milestones to reach their goals, and we hold them accountable to continuing down the path we've agreed upon.

"Do they just want to hold on to their job? That informs one way of leading someone – especially if they are not doing the core components of the role. They are endangering the only thing they hold dear. Do they want to have a larger role on the team? Do they want to be promoted? How can we work with them to construct a plan to achieve these things? It's important to hold each other accountable in these situations; construct a mutual plan and ensure that as the milestones are hit, your team member is on the proper trajectory to goal achievement.

"What sets me apart is I will do and have done whatever it takes to get the buy in of my teams, to have their backs, to communicate, be transparent, be responsive, be truthful. I've done it, I want to impart that wisdom and experience, and I want them on the journey with me.

"Ultimately, you can only go so far. You can lead the horse to water. You can't force them to drink, but you can show them why they should change based on what they indicated is their goal.

"Then there's the accountability component; that's why it's so important to track progress versus milestones. In your monthly meeting, pull out the previous month's notes and recap them. 'This is the conversation that we had last month. We talked about why you should make this change, what possible benefits that it would have. We agreed on a course of action.' Say they've made the change. 'Great job. Now let's work on this' - or, let's say they didn't make the change - 'Why? Where did we miss one another, because obviously we agreed that this was a good course of action? We wanted to avoid the trajectory that you are still on.'

"I think those are the most critical pieces of leadership and what is a lost art for many managers today who are slaves to spreadsheets or blindly follow an edict from above. Understand what motivates your people, let them be a part of the change, sell them on why change must occur, be transparent, help them reach their goals and have their backs."

"Pure gold," I said. "How do you make people feel important?"

"It's actually quite easy to make people feel good and make them feel special because they absolutely are. Everyone brings their own attributes; we collectively figure out how to match them to success in career - whatever that looks like.

"I think it's important to always look for ways that you can add value for them specifically, but make sure you're calling out just how appreciative you are of the value that they are adding as well. Make a concerted effort, even if it's just the most basic of e-mails or instant messages to check in, ask about something they have indicated is going on with them. Show you're listening. Show you care. Recognition matters. It goes a long way.

"Maybe they took a trip, are working on a project at their home, or they had a predicament with their kid. Their kid was sick, or they comment that they are having a tough time with a situation. Reference it and *check in* – people notice. Some people skip the pleasantries in e-mail or on calls, but I'm all for targeted pleasantries: don't drag on, but be a human. It's also a great way to stand out and be exemplary – most people won't lead off with any niceties but when you do, you'll make an impression. You'll add to your brand.

"And when people do excellent work, find a way to call it out – be it sending them a note copying their boss or finding a very public forum to call positive attention to them."

"You mentioned you're a busy guy – family, full-time, high-visibility gig at a big company, writing, speaking. How do you manage to not sacrifice quality to quantity, and juggle all of these priorities?"

"I love the question. I thought I was busy 10 years ago – people were calling me all the time. After hours, I was with my teams if I didn't have Elizabeth. Before her, I was my job.

"Eventually, at Majestech-Ware and CTMI, busyness reached fever pitch; I'd be triple- or quadruple-booked because I was poor at managing my schedule and priorities. There was an instant onslaught of a multitude of people and priorities vying for my time.

"I had to learn to take a step back and not get caught up in the fires or to take every meeting with everyone who wanted to talk to me. Most of them just wanted something from me; for me to give them leads, for me to put them in an account. People need to earn your time.

"I don't say that to be callous, but your time is the most valuable thing you have. Treat it like such. When you fail or you miss goal, the people who you gave all your time to won't answer for it. You will.

"How can I best impact my business and priorities today? What needs response? How can I move the ball down the field, either by inches or yards, on each opportunity? What are the high-level things; the non-negotiables?

"For me, it's God and family first. My faith, using my God-given talents to support and honor my family. Ensuring they are taken care of and knowing that I'm always putting them first and I'm physically with them as much as I can be.

"It's very important that I prioritize clients, my team and partners above all else in my job. We're all managers – we manage our book of business, our relationships in the sales food chain. Prospecting, driving, maintaining. It's really about coordination and orchestration of that team dynamic of colleagues, of other people that I'm working with day-to-day, but also of all resources that are available.

"Next, I've got meetings, calls and messages all day every day from different folks with varying levels of need. Some can impact their entire business, and others might be relatively minor comparatively, but they're all important. Sometimes even if I can provide a touch to the lower of the priorities, so the recipient knows I see it, I value them and I care, it achieves its purpose.

"But I operate in a fashion that ideally ensures that everyone who needs or wants me at least gets the response they deserve. And it's not to say I don't look back on my day sometimes and feel like I achieved absolutely nothing or was a failure to one or many of those people. Hopefully, I'll be granted a tomorrow."

"How specifically do you start a dialogue with business decision makers?"

"By acknowledging I'm not trying to hit the home run or sell the entire suite of services right out of the chute. I'm looking to forge a relationship – be it in the limited time I have of one call or over years. I'm there to be a representative of my brand but also a genuine human being; to add value. To offer and inform.

"It's selling a meeting to begin with. Why should this person take notice of me? Do we have something in common? Do I have access to something that will benefit them? I'm asking them for their most valuable commodity – time. So, it has to be perceived to be worth granting to me.

"Outreach or cold calling, sending e-mails, connecting via social media – it's all to get their attention. I cast a wide net to improve my odds. Then I sharpen my message to enhance odds even farther.

"Go with: 'I'd be interested in your thoughts on how this potential situation from your industry is addressed at your company.' 'I'd be interested in some of the priorities, projects and pain points that you're having.' 'I've just started working in this industry. I'd love to understand some of the things that are going well and how you see the landscape.' Ask to get their time based on popular, proven topics they will most likely want to talk about. Go in under the pretense of what they want to talk about, and you can blend in your priorities once you're across the table.

"If you recall, I told you about a survey I created, based on different conversations that I have found customers want to have; sending something like that to a decision maker and asking them what is top of mind for them has been helpful for me.

"Also, as we discussed before, presenting yourself as an advocate interested in ensuring they know all of the resources and support they are entitled to given their existing investment or standing can land you a meeting, too. People want to receive something and not always feel like they are being sold to.

"Start a conversation. Ask for advice. Don't necessarily go straight in and sound like every other salesperson that has come and failed with this prospect in the past. Frankly, if you sound like those who have failed before, you'll receive the same fate. That's why you want to differentiate yourself but add unique value.

"It's also not just about first contact. Often, I go considerable amounts of time without talking to clients, depending on the sales cycle and milestones. Then, it's about staying top of mind in a passive way. A 'quality marketing touch', if you will. Customers often want to digest things on their timetable, and they need to see our name 10 times before purchase. Be smart and effective about how those 10 times transpire. Say you send them an article and you say 'hey, what are your thoughts on this? I saw this, and I thought of the conversation we had.'

"Furthermore, just as we spoke before about leadership, you're leading these conversations and you are training a customer to make a decision based on a gap you've identified. You have to agree on the gap and a course of action to remedy it in order to advance the deal. Then, there are many other elements at play – what is their timeline? What is their budget? Are they the only decision-maker?

"Leadership and selling go hand in hand. You're coaching them and guiding them and convincing them to make a change.

"And every step of the way, you have to ensure you're bringing them on the journey with you. Starting the dialogue is one thing; agreeing on milestones another. Holding them accountable to those milestones, another still. It's just as important if not more so how you continue the conversation as opposed to how and that you start it. Don't call or e-mail to 'follow up' or 'check in' - you're always 'ensuring I'm respectful of the timelines you have established – what additional support or information may I provide?'

"Eventually, you'll get to a point where there can be mutual transparency and respect. They understand how to help you and you understand how to help them. Understand each other's fiscal year and budgeting cycles, how you can assist them with selling initiatives internally and make them look good, and they'll help you make deals when they count for you, too.

"Know your customers. It's the golden rule."

"How do you keep motivated? How do you keep others motivated?"

Vincent laughed, ever so slightly. "It's a long game. But it's comprised of moments and steps. I once had legendary motivation – I was called a bull in a china shop. No matter what, I always bounced back and was always animated and energetic and positive.

"I don't care who you are, there's a breaking point. You will tire. A prized stallion cannot run full speed race after race with no rest. And the politics, the bureaucracy, the constant challenges and setbacks – they will eventually wear at you. Even if you're able to disguise it from others, it will be there.

"Motivation is about what makes people tick. I've had a lot of motivating forces over the years. Making my parents proud, then making money, then getting promoted... again and again. It can be competition, it can be keeping up with the Joneses. It can evolve, or devolve, into keeping your job or just getting through the day.

"We all have goals. Some are elaborate and some are very simple. Some people want to take over the world and others merely wish to maintain a certain standard of living.

"I guess what I'm saying is personally and professionally, I've been all over the board as far as what my current motivating factors are. I'm intrinsically wired to do the best I can in every scenario. In the past, I've run at 100% of capacity without any signs of slowing. In recent years, I've been substantially less – but likely no one knew it. Fortunately, my 70% looks better than the 100% of others. So I'm told.

"As for motivating others, I just become their promoter – plain and simple. It's not about coming in and forcing change; change will happen naturally if there is a mutually beneficial relationship. The same can be said of the client relationship – it's the sales food chain. The circle of life. I'm not 'motivating' anything – I'm understanding what's important to my target audience, I'm showing them why a change or why my way is better than what they're doing now, and I'm tying it to what matters most to them – more money, more job security, a promotion. Whatever it is.

"I've stood in a room of hundreds and delivered daily stand-up's and division meetings. Every one of them had to be unique, focused solely on moving them to do something different. Something more. Something better.

"Getting motivation is one thing. Keeping it is something else entirely. Consistency is everything, and you cannot get consistent results without consistent leadership - especially regaining it in the face of lost momentum. Sure, there were times our results faltered, I wasn't happy and my reaction or response was to fly off the handle or start pointing fingers. Fortunately, that was in my 20's. People want to be valued, treated with respect. To feel secure. To know they can have a bad day, week or month and you're not going to rip away their security. At the same time, being respectful and transparent and real when it comes to results and expectations and timelines is important. I've never fired anybody that didn't know well in advance it was coming.

"Obsess over people and process, not results. The results will come as a result of the right people doing the best process."

78

"So, I have to ask – what was missing when you missed goal?"

Vincent didn't blink nor did he miss a beat. "The wrong people had zero process. No consistency, completely reactive business model. It was night and day difference from one year to the next."

"And how were your results?"

"We're getting there," he smiled. "Do you want to see my office before we go?"

"Sure!" I said. I had heard CTMI/Majestech-Ware had an incredible center here in Minneapolis. And I was right.

Coffee cups in hand, I followed Vincent down a corridor to the elevators. Just this building alone was beautiful and very modern; officially in Downtown West near the Metrodome, CTMI occupied a large suite encompassing the fifth floor.

Off the elevators, Vincent led me into the suite; he greeted and was greeted by a number of people including the administrative assistants, a handful of enthusiastic gentlemen in suits, he garnered waves from a few folks in meetings from behind their glass walls, and numerous employees.

"How long has this place been here?"

"34 years," he replied, "but it was remodeled and re-opened two years ago after the acquisition."

Vincent proceeded to walk me through the event spaces, the technology labs, the developer space, the demo hub and the very modernized workspaces for employees. It was very modern, very cutting edge.

"Do you come here a lot?" I inquired.

"A few times a week. Between meetings and occasionally just needing a space for a podcast interview where there isn't a constantly barking dog, I love having this place here."

"I'm impressed," I commented.

"Ready for the next stop on the tour?" he inquired.

"Let's do it."

We made for the exits; prior to reaching the elevators, Vincent was stopped no fewer than three times by people eager to talk to him about what they wanted from him. They feigned small talk, which he handled dispassionately.

We then made our way to the elevators, out of the building and to the parking garage and his waiting Aston Martin.

It had transformed into a sunny day, yet the air was still cool. He put the top down and had a playlist of classic rock.

"We're going to do a little bit of a drive," Vincent prefaced. "But then I'll swing back into town for a dinner before taking you to your flight. Sound good?"

"I'm game, provided you give me the whole story," I laughed, prompting him to continue.

"What do you want to know next?"

"You mentioned the first quarter of fiscal year 2018, new leadership, the TGI deal and driving a ton of pipeline. How did that all wind up?"

Chapter 6 – Blast from the Past

We drove I-494 westbound, away from downtown Minneapolis. The speed limit was 60 and Vincent's Aston Martin pushed 70. The top was down, and it was just windy enough to conjure a breeze. It was now a perfect day.

Our path took us alongside the Minnesota River and past exits for North Corridor Park and Anderson Lake on our way through Bloomington and Eden Prairie. We eventually reached MN 55.

"If I had to sum up my first year in role, under Quintana, it was a lot of learning on the fly. There was no support and a significant amount of unfinished business and deals left on the table. I truly learned the amount of time it would take to construct the types of deals I needed to be making. I also learned that everyone wants to be involved in the deal with you to get deal credit, but not everyone actually wants to contribute; I'd have to do a lot of the heavy lifting on my own. Now I knew how to lift.

"Year Two was an all-out blitz. I lost some accounts to the Large Business Group and also had some slip to Small Business. Foolishly, I tried to keep some of the ones that fell down but only did it because of a good relationship; I got tagged with needless quota that I got burned by. From that, I learned that I should – most of the time – let the chips fall where they may. To not spin my wheels trying to chase stuff that may not benefit me. I was, however, able to keep a credit-card processing company that paid dividends.

"I did feel a lot more prepared and knowledgeable in 2018 than the year prior – that's for sure. Definitely developed some good relationships with my team. I had learned who I could count on and which situations would require me to do more of the driving. Knowing that is quite valuable.

"That time was also defined by a conscious effort I made to do more with others; I played some golf with Nick Aragon. We even won a partner golf tournament we played in. Abby, the kids and I would go to Nick's house and spend time with his wife and kids. We had them over a few times. Went hiking with my father-in-law Dan Winters. Jeff Mason visited Minneapolis with his family and they stopped by our house. We hung out at my bar and had a great time.

"Elizabeth turned 10 and I actually felt that relationship going the opposite direction – she was more into her friends and her own stuff than being my best buddy anymore. I teared up the first time she wanted to walk to the bus stop by herself. But that's life. It's inevitable.

"I also had a fair amount of travel. But all in all, I bounced back and forth between hesitant confidence and starting to understand things and being depressed, feeling out of place. My relationships with everyone in my family were evolving, I was now the unintended sole income and I felt disconnected from the home front because I had to work all the time and got only a little bit of evening with them.

"My family also took another hit when John Propst, the man who had dated my Grandma since a year after Grandpa died in 2001, died that fall of 2017. He was a really nice man; never pretended to be anything more than that for our family, but I've certainly noticed in the years since I've seen far less of my extended family – even for holidays."

"Man, I'm so sorry to hear that," I acknowledged. "I remember how your Grandpa's death rocked the family and I know John was a positive force."

"Yeah - it was definitely another blow, but not unforeseen.

"I also just kind of threw myself into activities and mindset that would complement the 'man on fire' persona I had adopted. I got my hair cut super short again for the first time in nearly five years. I started writing a ton more articles, which got me noticed by major podcast hosts and interviewed on their shows. For the first time in a long time, I was having people come up to me at events that referenced my writing and my sales persona and knew who I was. It felt good.

"To put it into perspective, Year One I took it on the chin. Year Two I built a foundation – based on deals I chased or closed in Year One added to prospecting I did in Year Two. I was getting meetings with people I had never met, using the questionnaire that got me recognized, and bringing in my technical data specialist – Prens Koruyucu – to every door I opened. I could get the meeting and then I brought the smart people in, and handed deals off to Mick Logan when I needed a vendor. The dream team. My maniacal follow-up and pipeline management did the rest.

"I also have to credit Jordan Waters; he had also moved on to a new role with the new fiscal year, but was my GM for a year. He is the one I had to work with to escalate my complaint on Quintana because he was her boss at the time. And while he was not really able to do much to help me because he had moved to another role, he continued monthly mentorship calls with me. And he shared with me that he had once gotten a poor appraisal and no bonus – and bounced back the next year to be Manager of the Year. I still talk to him regularly to this day.

"The TGI deal was the talk of the town for most of the year; I had to do a write up for the CTMI CEO on it. But I wasn't going to pin my year on the hopes of that thing panning out. There were additional data deals with a dozen other accounts, growth with the gym management company FitSmart, and new deals or potential deals with a company that did food service for schools, a pharmaceutical organization, a start-up who tracked hospital surgical equipment, a large hotel chain, a machinery company, a large retailer – they all needed data management.

"It was funny – I heard from others that the word on the street was that I was killing it. That I was a rock star. But because of what Quintana did to me, I didn't believe it or was skeptical. I still didn't let up. I couldn't. I kept going at 100% of capacity all day, every day. My new team and my boss – Jeremy Rivers – were extremely well-regarded in the business unit and now I was the star.

"I really liked Jeremy. His attitude was infectious. He's pick a 'DJ of the week' for his Monday morning conference calls, and someone from the prior week – based on results or pipeline, or whatever metrics he selected – would pick a song to play on the call. I won often.

"He understood the business and knew the game really, really well. He was a master of positioning himself as a client advocate, of understanding the ins and outs of our process, and he knew that the sale and the relationships were very important. But where he shined even brighter was knowing how to negotiate, how to use levers like funding dollars and incentives and working the licensing in an advantageous way. He was truly a master of the game, which is what I wanted to be.

"My team was pretty cool, too, and more and more folks on the team would reach out to me asking me for ideas, bouncing ideas off me and asking me how I drove so much pipeline. I talked a lot with guys on the new team like Johnny Smythe, Dave Anthony, Steve Kirkpatrick and Will Matthews. They would talk to me like I was well respected, like I had great ideas. Again, I still felt the stigma from Quintana, so I didn't trust it. I didn't feel worthy of the praise or hype – even though I had been a star before. It was probably a good thing – because I had no ability to get over-confident.

"I just wanted to live up to that hype. And the job didn't ever get any easier.

"I lost a substantial deal at the pharmaceutical company to a competitor. In hindsight, I should have controlled it more – but I really didn't have the experience at that point in deals of that ilk; it required custom solutions to be built on top of our platform, there was another vendor involved and I didn't know enough to take control. I got very little support from the territory sales team on the deal.

"There was a notable streaming service where I prospected a deal as well; they would be tracking data on the different industries they serviced and we were part of an RFP process. The initial deal was not large, but the potential upside was good. I had Merit Productivity and Mick in there to compete on our behalf so they could win the services and support business. I did my part. Or, so I thought.

"Days before the RFP was due, Merit just bailed on me and I had to find a different vendor. It really left me in a bind. They claimed they didn't quite have the level of proficiency, which is knowledge I would have benefited from previously. Then, they ditched me on another 'small potatoes' customer. Mick assured me it was not on account of him; his leadership only wanted to go after 'the big things.' I think it was suddenly lost on them that they won't get the big things if they don't help me with the 'little things' and I was the one feeding them every deal they got in the Twin Cities. That was a big red flag. It also was the first sign I'd need to find some fresh blood.

"Then it was a problem with FitSmart; they were going to bite off on a pilot for us to revamp their entire platform, modernize and automate it. There was a devices component and they would be rolling the platform out to more gyms. The deal was supposed to be done in early 2017. It kept dragging and dragging; FitSmart was positioning themselves to be bought, and at the end of 2017 they were – and the new company wanted nothing to do with us.

"If I had to sum up the first half of our fiscal year it's characterized by a lot of travel and trying to drive as much pipeline as humanly possible. Then, the back half of the year, you have to be laser-focused to get every deal closed. It's a fight to the finish.

"The travel would consist of companywide events, trade shows and partner events. I'd have to go to Dallas often, occasionally Vegas because we had a multi-year deal with them. Chicago sometimes. Sometimes D.C. where CTMI was headquartered.

"The primary difference in the makeup of my business travel now as opposed to years past is my behavior - I was early to bed, early to rise and in the gym. Instead of going out partying, I'd be Skyping my wife and kids. I can only play the game so much these days, and I'm cognizant most 'friendships' in the business game are fake. I have some true friends from it all, but they are a rare find.

"I also had really turned into the guy who had to play the villain to different vendors, specifically if I was replacing them on an account – meaning I was to blame nearly everywhere I went. Customers told vendors that I was the one who recommended a different vendor, even if they asked me to. Any vendor whose relationship at an account went dark blamed me by default. It was thankless.

"Vendors kept me at arm's length until they wanted something or wanted me to insert them into accounts they couldn't break into. At least they were always good for a free lunch. But they weren't willing to do the hustle, the prospecting or the execution. I found out Year One that unless I led the entire process, few – if any – would get the job done. Only Mick, frankly, and Merit had already started to clamp down on his eagerness to put me first in favor of blindly chasing really big deals they couldn't land.

"Most of our inside sales and specialist resources were similar – I'd find pipeline for them and they still wouldn't drive the sale forward. I had to do it, and of course they wanted credit when the deal got done. They'd all pat themselves on the back for the win, but few of them really contributed or did much other than throw up obstacles.

"Senior leadership would tell us to 'raise your hand and everyone you need will swarm the deal' to help you - it was a joke. I tried to get – ironically – one of Quintana's new technical specialists to help me on TGI because the deal potential was so big, and she tried to block me rather than help me. She came up with three reasons why her team couldn't help me. I went over her head and finally won.

"Everything is a struggle. So many broken or non-existent processes and fake people. So much time spent with minutia and administrative tasks that take away from getting the job done and delivering for our customers."

"I'm struggling here, Vincent," I interjected. "I'm not seeing a lot of redeeming qualities. Why do you do it?"

Vincent considered his response for a moment. He looked at me, and also took in his surroundings.

"For starters, you're sitting in it. And you're looking at it. Hustle to pay the bills, and side hustle to feed my soul. I do have freedom when I really need it. Nobody's breathing down my neck – not right now.

"Most other internal roles, I'd be bored to tears. Something external, I have to start all over again and re-build my brand. If I go to a vendor, no matter how much they pay me, I forfeit prestige. Thanks to my books and podcasts, I've talked to people all over the world about sales and leadership – which is *what I really enjoy doing*... but that doesn't pay the bills."

"Couldn't it, though?"

"I don't know," he answered truthfully. "I left sales management when I went to the Downey management consultant firm and was stung from that experience. I could start my own thing, but I'd need people and funding and things I know nothing about. There is a part of me that wants the structure, but to be able to run free when I want to; that's why I was so successful in the brand new Regional Manager gig I took at Majestech-Ware a few years back. Of course, all good things come to an end. I was happiest when I was running the ABM advertising division."

"And that's not a place you could return to."

"I wouldn't want to at this point. That division was bankrupted and sold three times over. What I ran doesn't exist anymore. I could never re-create it. But it doesn't mean I'm over it."

There was momentary silence.

"I saw Keith Dickhauser that winter, actually. I took Abby to a comedy show, and I'm out in the lobby getting refreshments and there he was. I couldn't avoid him; I walked right into him, practically, and he more or less boxed me in. He was a close-talker, and he had had too much to drink already."

"Oh, wow – how did that go? How did that *feel?*"

"It started out...OK. But it relatively quickly descended into weird. Awkward. I realized that I had made so much progress in my life since then and he was very stuck in the past.

"He asked a lot of the same questions over and over again; like how he was portrayed in *Birth of a Salesman*. I could tell he was pretty unhappy about it, which makes sense because he used to talk to people about it after I was gone. He made references to it several times – like I had gone after him.

86

"It started calmly enough. He did ask how I was; I told him I was married with two girls, got my dream car. Told him I had been in management with Majestech-Ware for some time. You know, of course I consciously threw around stuff that showed I had eclipsed what I was in 2010. It was nice to really be in such a better position personally and professionally.

"He said he retired in 2015 from ABM, which I know he was forced to do because of the magnitude of the complaints against him. He just got one too many HR cases filed. He very easily recalled timelines – that it had been 7 years since we last saw each other, that he thinks about that time all the time and remembers it like it was yesterday.

"I told him I know I was a kid then and had to grow up. I was trying to be nice. He acknowledged I was immature and he was a jerk and it could have been handled better. He seemed somewhat open and gracious when we first started talking.

"As the conversation continued, though, it deteriorated; he started saying it had been other people who had been responsible for taking me out. He cited Danny Boyd, his clerical manager, as the one who was solely responsible for turning me into HR for a personal text message to someone who didn't report to me – obviously, now my wife. He said he and Lydia Rawlings, the HR Director, called up to the VP and he's the one who insisted I be terminated – even though it should never have been on his radar. Keith claimed he said it was all BS and asked for another chance for me.

"Truth is, I didn't care. Number one, I had people willing to testify in court that Keith bragged about what he did to me and threatened them with the same fate if they didn't fall in line or if they tried to help me. That's why I won.

"Second - I just kept telling Keith, 'That's fine,' or 'It doesn't matter to me anymore – it was another lifetime ago' and nodding. Because it's true. Nothing he could have said short of 'I'm sorry' would have made a bit of difference to me in that moment."

"Do you hate him?"

"No," he answered quickly. "Not anymore.

"I tried to walk away a couple of times, with the excuse I still needed to get drinks. Finally, the lobby lights flashed so we knew the show was about to start; but he kept talking. He started repeating himself, asking me what I do now for a living.

He never was any good at actually listening to anybody. He just liked to hear himself talk.

"He wanted my business card and asked for it multiple times; fortunately, I didn't have any on me. He asked multiple times if I would have lunch with him. Talk man to man. And then he would start cursing, clearly upset about the memories this was conjuring up for him.

"I was talking about the present and he kept talking about the past. Funny because it was years before I could finally let it all go. There's a part of me that died at 31 and lost all the years until 39; there's a part of me that will never get over feeling like I was at the top of the mountain, making an impact on hundreds of professionals all at the same time – live and in person. A feeling I have not recaptured since.

"The longer the conversation with Keith, the madder he got about my book. He just kept talking about it. I was angry when you interviewed me for it, but it was how it all happened from my point of view. But I told Keith that I don't care about the past anymore. To top it all off, one of our old reps – Jamie Sonse – actually saw us talking there, came up and marveled, 'Wow, this is quite the reunion.'

"So - yeah – I saw Keith again. He told me he had seen me 6 months prior at Oceana Restaurant. He was with a customer, he said, and thought about talking to me.

"He said he would swear on a stack of Bibles - 'I'm Roman Catholic' he said – that he tried to save me. But whatever. I knew Danny Boyd was part of the plot. But who would have involved our VP? Why did Lydia – head of HR – tell me point blank she supported me, and this case had no merit?

"Bottom line is this: I was an untrained, uncoached, unpolished kid who made a lot of mistakes. I surely could have been fired for other things, but what they did to me was illegal. I won in court in the end and it's over. I don't care.

"I hated the fact that momentarily that meeting with Keith Dickhauser unsettled me because it made me think about and re-think about some of the stuff I had laid to rest long ago.

"I want to remember it only for the beginning of the conversation. Look, I knew Dickhauser for 5 years before all of that went down. He was a big part of my career and success. He did give me a chance. He told me that night that I was the most talented person he had ever met. He called me 'the rock star' and cited all of the stand-up's I had done and the elaborate e-mails and my leads and auto-dialer process.

"Some of the conversation was really positive. He said he respected me so much. But he unearthed one of his famous lines, 'I don't hold grudges,' which I found so ironic considering he held them worse than anyone I've ever known. I watched the guy retaliate against anyone who tried to stand up to him, and finally he eliminated me for siding against him when his butt was on the line.

"Was anything he said true? I don't believe that if he had tried to save me that he would have been unsuccessful. Heck, my successes were always shielded by the fact he didn't want me overshadowing my peer and his buddy, Mark Rogers.

"The reason I got fired was a completely personal thing, and frankly anyone could have seen that.

"I told him I had learned a lot from the situation, and he actually asked what I had learned. I told him I learned I had to separate the friendships from the business. I lost every one of those friendships, including what was once a friendship with him. I had thought a lot of those people cared about me at the time. Come to find out, none of them did.

"Haven't heard a thing from him since. That was three years ago."

"Wow. Sounds bittersweet. Good to get the closure, I suppose, but I doubt it was fun thinking about that stuff again."

"It was fleeting. It was inevitable, I suppose, that I'd run into him again. It certainly was good to hear him say some of the nice things, to realize I had moved forward and improved myself. But to hear the bitterness and anger amidst my apathy – what a difference the years had made.

"It honestly doesn't help that I still don't feel whole. Like I beat them, but I didn't win. I would give anything to have back what I had then – exactly. I say that, but under the surface, I didn't have what I thought I had. These people who I thought were my friends only wanted something from me and they dropped me at the first sign of trouble. The division isn't what it was, so even if I went back it would never be the same. It was one moment in time.

"So, I struggle with meaning and purpose. My animosity toward Quintana fueled me after she tried to destroy me, but the reality was that always in my mind –

sometimes in the back and sometimes at the forefront – my thought was 'what in the world is the next move?'

"ABG made another play for me. I had some people try to convince me to apply for the Large Business Group doing the same thing I did; then I heard from a partner that their general manager Stefan Adams was looking for someone young and moldable and he had gotten garbage reviews on me – from Quintana. That's the kind of stuff that haunts me.

"There was really nowhere else I could go – not where I wouldn't have to start all over, reinvent myself, or sacrifice the prestige of CTMI. And so I just trudged on. Call after call. Report after report. Day after day. I would look at the date every morning in the bottom right corner of my computer screen, focus on it, and think only of how I could maximize that day.

"And my fiscal year 2018 – while it started with a flurry of activity and positive attention for incredible pipeline growth, hit a rough patch. I had a 59% October 2017 – it was completely out of my control. Just deal cycles. But I was hovering at 84% nearly halfway through the year with the biggest quota months ahead.

"I was also getting sucked into a lot of non-revenue generating activity. Some I could avoid, some I couldn't. The big pharmaceutical company that Large Business Group dumped on me was used to a lot of attention; they were managed before at a 7:1 ratio of customers to account manager. We were managing at a 200:1 ratio. I had to do a lot of damage control over our span of control and to manage their expectations when they wanted literally daily calls with our team. It just wasn't feasible."

"How did you finesse that one?" I queried.

"I found a specialist from every single business group we had," he replied. "Got them all on a call with the customer. There were 13 folks on from CTMI, including me. I wowed them by showing them all of the people who supported their account. Then I made sure they knew that I would selectively pull these folks in for subsequent conversations given the content and customer need. But now, they had a roster and I could spread out the work.

"I also got saddled with the infamous OV Group – *after* they had bought everything I sold them that another team got paid for and now that they carried an additional $1.2 million quota I'd never hit. Quintana's curse just kept doling out the punishment."

We passed Medina Golf & Country Club. It was a beautiful day; there were numerous players on the course wearing their classy golf polos and slacks.

"How do you manage all of these uncertain situations? How do you get customers to adhere to timelines when sales cycles are literally all over the place?"

Vincent laughed. "You just do your best. Seriously.

"I'll tell you – all of this stuff is uncertain. I think it's funny, looking back, how vendors and my team and I thought certain customers would be our big bets and they went bust, and yet we found these diamonds in the rough that gave us banner years.

"You just have to keep a balanced approach, no matter the turbulence; no matter the noise," he said, with a worldly air that added credibility. "It's why I try to have so many quality touches in the territory – I never know when someone will go dark or a deal will go sideways. I can't bank on a deal to happen. I can only control the fact that I try to drive and maintain and nurture so many relationships. I can control how enticing I make the deal. I can control how much value I bring to the table, how many resources and people I engage for it and how much I'm willing to give to get what my company and I want and need.

"Holding the other party accountable is tricky but key; getting them to agree to the next steps and timelines, sending a thorough recap, and – when you make subsequent touches to keep the ball in play – ensuring you make it about *them*.

"Say 'To be respectful of your established timeline' or 'our mutually established timeline, I wanted to ensure we maintain momentum' on this item or that item; articulating fully the steps that have to occur and the dates by which they have to occur – you lay it all out there and you have to constantly guide them to the destination. It won't happen on your desired timeline, but with appropriate measures you can get them nearly all the way there so they can make the decision to buy.

"Eventually, once you've got a deal taking form, you have to provide incentives for early closure or deadlines for action that have repercussions if they're missed. Deal points or your additional reinvestment or some resources are contingent on moving on certain components or signing by a certain date. Again – you can't force their hand, but you certainly want to ethically control as many

91

aspects and motivate them in any way you can. Both in favor of the deal happening and to prevent missing out if steps are missed."

"Did you do that with Trucking Group International?"

Vincent laughed. "Mike Jericho moved milestones on me like it was nobody's business. More audibles had to be called on that deal than any I've ever done. I'd spend countless hours crafting a presentation and having my team spend time with his as research so we could competently present to him and his senior leadership only to have him inexplicably cancel on me just a day or two prior."

"Sounds pretty classless – what do you do?

"What *can* you do? I'd leave him a message and e-mail him back, iterating just how much time our team had spent in preparation on work for him and his team, the feedback we were getting from his employees and why we felt it so pertinent. Stuff like that may fall on deaf ears. He certainly didn't appear to be moved, and knowing him he likely relished the fact he had wasted our time.

"But if you chase every single deal like it's the most important deal, you will win some. And that will be good enough.

"I had found my 'dream team' and I entered a zone. I knew what I was good at, and I was lining up meetings and calls and going in with my Technical Data Specialist, Prens Koruyucu to uncover new opportunities and then I'd hand them to Mick Logan at Merit and I'd move on and drum up more. It was really starting to work. The setbacks were inevitable, but if I could just rinse and repeat, a rhythm of business and revenue could be formed.

"My new boss, Jeremy Rivers, asked me to serve on a social selling team representing our business unit. Most of the folks on those calls really didn't know social selling the way I knew it; many were millennials who had a social media presence; others had an established LinkedIn profile, but none really knew how to leverage them at scale to make new relationships that turned into deals. We'd get on these calls, and I talked about what I did, and it just blew these folks away.

"I think a lot of people worry about 'spamming.' They feel that sending connection requests to people they don't know is some form of spam. You know what? Like anything, it can certainly be done a right way and a wrong way. Blind connection requests are absolutely a waste. But targeted, focused connection requests with a specific intent, personalized verbiage and a goal of connection –

92

rather than selling something – are a value add. That has been the driving force of how I've used these tools. And that is how I frame it when I train it.

"Our social selling committee was tasked with putting together a demo video for the channel and everyone on the team was supposed to contribute pieces to it. When it came down to the day we were making it, only 3 team members of 15 showed up, nobody had anything prepared, and they were just talking in circles about how this needed to be done and what were we going to do?

"So, I just took charge. I told them I'd share my screen and start a recording, and I just walked through a day in the life of how I prospect. It was that simple.

"And that video became *infamous* within CTMI and Majestech-Ware. It was shared broadly, catching the attention of senior executives.

"Very similarly to my ABM days when my boss Derek Walters had to step away to help another local sales office and nobody but me volunteered to take on extra responsibilities – *those are the moments when you can take on more, shine, get noticed and get promoted.* If a need exists, and you take a unique approach to fill a gap that has visibility, your brand will be enhanced exponentially.

"Some of the people I talked to like Jeremy Rivers or his boss Janet Leary or Jordan Waters would reference that I had come off a 'tough year' but the reality was I had achieved 14% growth in the territory and signed a ton of new logos. I just hadn't gotten anything but flak for it. The 'tough year' was really more in the repeat harassment and subsequent black mark.

"Now I was being treated like I was a superstar from out of nowhere. It was like I was making an ascent toward a second career peak. And it felt good. I had never felt anything quite like this.

"One difference this time is that I was humble. Instead of standing in front of groups of people taking credit or calling myself great, I was going out of my way to recognize people on my team who were doing great work – like my Technical Data Specialist Prens Koruyucu, like Nate Gammons my business app specialist. I was drawing positive attention to these folks and making them get noticed more, which – in turn – made them work harder in support of me.

"Prens and I were making such names for ourselves that his boss – Jason Quartz – and his boss's boss, the VP Maury Bobrick – even hopped on some of our calls to listen to us work our magic. Jason was telling people I was one of the best in the business – a far cry from the condemnation Quintana served up.

"*This* is what I had been fighting for. I was suddenly being heralded as the star. And I was doing it right this time.

"It bothered me that the new Director in Large Business Group made that comment about wanting someone 'young and moldable' over me, based on bad intel from Quintana – made me feel old, washed up and like the trash Quintana had made me out to be. But I was winning over people like Jordan, Janet, Jason Quartz, Jeremy Rivers.

"Not everybody is going to like me – that's fair. What was so hard to swallow was that I was so much better – of a person, of a professional, of a leader – than who I was a decade ago and yet I was still facing sometimes seemingly insurmountable challenges.

"That said, I knew I could not let one terrible manager's negative opinion of me either become true or affect my attitude or performance or alter the perception for those who believe I shine.

"It also stuck with me, seeing Dickhauer again, because all of those old memories and feelings shot back to the surface.

"But I had to look forward. I still had a long way to go on the road back."

We were driving through Greenfield and entered Rockford. I guessed in my mind where we were going.

Chapter 7 – You Can Go Home Again

Not far from Lake Rebecca Park, we entered the lot of a three-story building just off Highway 55.

Vincent pulled his Aston Martin into the lot, his eyes not wavering much from the building.

"This is where it all began," he muttered.

"The Rockford call center?" I asked, knowing the answer.

"Yes. My first ABM sales gig. I started here in 2001. Haven't set foot in the place since 2006."

"Really? You never went back?"

"Not for a few reasons," he answered, shaking his head almost ashamed. He pulled into a parking spot not far from the entrance. The lot was relatively full, but he parked off to the side where he was not next to another vehicle. "When I first left for ABM Advertising, a lot of the reps here tried to jump ship and come work for me. Some were successful. It caused some tension and bad blood between the managers here and me. I did very little – admittedly – to quell their anger. In fact, I basically fueled and relished it.

"After ABM took me out in 2010, I certainly never made it back. I was persona non grata for quite a time. I was ironically in my old Greenfield office in 2015; it was bought by a client of ours at Majestech-Ware and I had to go for a training event. That was surreal – seeing the entire place modified, updated but setting foot where my former office had been. But I haven't set foot in this building in 13 years."

We got out of the car, shut our doors, and he paused briefly – just taking it all in.

"Does this take you back?" I asked.

He laughed. "It actually makes me think about all of the times I had to make this trek, hungover, from my apartment, weaving through traffic in just 10 minutes or so in order to arrive on time. I don't know how I did it, honestly."

I chuckled. "We've all been there."

We walked toward the front door. There were some people filing out as it was nearing the lunch hour.

"Vincent!" one of them exclaimed. "Vincent Scott!"

Vincent turned to face her.

"Lacy!" he exclaimed. They embraced. "How in the world are you?"

"I'm good," she replied. "What are you doing here?"

"Just grabbing lunch with Danny and Chris. Catching up. Figured I'd check out the old digs."

"You haven't been back in..."

"Yeah, 13 years," he completed her thought. "This is Carson Heady, by the way. He and I go way back."

"Nice to meet you," I expressed.

"Likewise," Lacy stated, extending her hand. I took it and we shook.

"Vincent is being modest," I said. "I'm actually writing about him."

"That's who you are," she said. "I thought your name sounded familiar. Well, he is the best manager I've ever had. And that's saying something, because this place has been a revolving door of them.

"He saved my hide once upon a time. Well, probably many times, but he's the only reason I'm still here. I was going through tough times and got caught by our Director sneaking services onto a customer's account without saying anything to them. Vincent convinced me to do the opposite of what I was planning on doing; he told me to completely throw myself at the mercy of the court rather than trying to defend myself or act like I hadn't done it or play dumb. To expose some of my personal problems to the Director that she would be able to relate to.

"And he was right. They suspended me and I was on probation, but I kept my job. The Director told me she had every intention of firing me, but my honesty is what saved me. That was 14 years ago. I've been here 20 years this year. And it never would have happened without Vincent."

"Wow - what a story," I exclaimed. "What a guy!" I said, turning to Vincent and holding my hands up in emphasis.

"You're too kind," he said. "I was just trying to be a human being."

96

"That's a lost art," Lacy said. "I've never had a manager before or since that cared as much as you did. Thank you."

"Don't mention it." Vincent changed the subject, clearly uncomfortable taking compliments, "How's the boys?"

"Taylor is 18 and Tanner is 14," she replied. Vincent looked shocked.

"My gosh," he responded. "Unbelievable. I remember when Taylor was a toddler and when Tanner was born. How's Randy?"

"He's good. We were just talking about you the other day, and how we used to go for the unlimited margaritas at El Taco Riendo."

"Yes!" Vincent exclaimed. "I loved that place. Haven't been there in years."

"Well, I have to get something to eat and back or you know there's hell to pay," Lacy said.

"Some things never change."

"Give us a call sometime," Lacy said, both of them knowing that it likely would not happen. "We've got to all get together again."

"That sounds nice," Vincent said as they embraced once more.

Lacy left. Vincent and I continued into the building.

There were small offices on both sides of the immense hallway, leading to a stairway. Potted plants were on both sides of what was a red and beige carpet that led to the stairs.

"Man, this looks totally different," Vincent recounted. "None of these offices were in business. The color scheme has totally changed."

We ascended the staircase. From the stairs, you could see into a small conference room where the blinds were half-drawn. A computer table, a round table in the middle and chairs were the primary props and the walls were adorned in a white board and posters advertising ABM products.

"The Aquarium," Vincent said, smiling.

"Where all the call monitoring and disciplinary meetings were conducted, right?" I asked.

"Good memory," Vincent said. "We had a ton of meetings in there. Team meetings, too. Shelly Cheekwood and I went toe to toe in there many a time."

Shelly had been Vincent's manager – the Area Manager of the call centers in Rockford and Montrose – from 2002 until 2007. She had her fair share of issues in her personal life that bled into work, was often absentee during her tenure and at the peak of her flakiness she and Vincent were at odds frequently.

It was the age-old story: Vincent's managers were intimidated by his skill and following, and Vincent did very little to gain consensus and their advocacy. He just accepted the leadership role the office wanted him to take, alienating Shelly and making their relationship quite strained. Shelly then backed others for promotions within the division and while Vincent finally got one of his own, he had to leave the entire business unit to get it.

At the top of the stairs, Vincent pressed the buzzer to the right of the door. Peering in, we could see rows of cubicles and more posters.

A girl appeared, walking toward the door. When she saw Vincent, her mouth opened wide in shock and she smiled. She opened the door and let us enter.

"Oh my gosh, Vincent!" she shrieked, embracing him. "How are you?"

"I'm good, Elise. Great to see you," he replied.

"Hi," Elise said, extending her hand to me. We introduced ourselves to each other.

"Elise was in my training class. We started September 17, 2001. There were 12 people in our class, and we're the only 2 who made it out," Vincent told me.

"Holy cow!" I said. "And you're still here!"

"18 years," she said.

"We didn't have a choice," Vincent recalled. "We were the only reps from off the street. The others mostly retreated into previous roles they had in the company because they didn't want to do the job. We stuck it out."

"There were many times I almost left," Elise said. "But as I got older and my husband lost his job, I was the bread-winner. The money and benefits were very important. So, I've stayed."

"What's it like these days?" Vincent asked.

"It's changed a lot. When you were here is when we switched from commercial to consumer. We picked up additional states and responsibilities. There was a time when they had a ton of different departments. Then we had to do just

98

about every possible job function out of this center and they closed offices that did others. Now they have us trying to retain customers and either upsell or move them into different phone, Internet and cable packages."

"I'm guessing telephone sales aren't what they used to be," Vincent mused.

We chatted briefly as we walked out toward the cubicles. Looking left, there was a hallway next to the series of cubicles that led into a large lunchroom. Straight back – beyond cubicles – was the window overseeing the city street. To the right, another hallway wrapped around to an entire office floor of cubicles. There was a small opening against the right-hand wall where there were sofas and chairs.

"That's new," Vincent noticed. Then, he surveyed the scene, walking up to the first cubicle coming up on his left.

"They moved all of the manager cubes to the back and the reps are now up front," Elise said.

"This used to be my spot," Vincent told me, beaming proudly. "My team was – at one time – these first couple of rows. Then we expanded to the first 9 rows." He waved his hand in that direction.

"And I was always on your team," Elise announced proudly. "No matter how many times we changed."

"Yeah," Vincent said. "There were lots of changes. We started with 6 on our team, and eventually had 37. It was the biggest team in the company. And had I stayed, it would have been even more."

"Why did you take on that many?" I asked.

"Because I knew I could. And because some full offices were not much bigger. I was trying to prove I could manage that many people all by myself while Dick Knoll – my primary frenemy and rival here – got promoted and had 3 managers of his own running an office of 51. Before I left, I was actually in talks to take a team of 52 for that very reason."

I laughed. Typical Vincent Scott.

"They wouldn't allow it, though. Dana Warsaw – our Director who most people just called 'The Saw' because she terminated people like it was a bodily function – told me she wouldn't let me take on a larger team until I fired someone based on her scripted call flow process. I simply wouldn't comply."

"Why?" I inquired.

"People can have a bad day," he responded. "People do their best work when they're not worried about their boss dinging them for every detail of a call. Even the best sellers in that environment – myself included – can have a call that doesn't hit 85% of their script in a day featuring over 100 calls. In exchange for cutting my team slack, I expected exemplary results. If they performed, they got a pass – within reason. If they didn't, I investigated. It's constant checks and balances, but I treated them like people.

"I'd also gift them time off the phones for achieving certain metrics. If they were taking care of me – things that boosted my number – I would reciprocate with giving them some time off here or there. I always looked for ways to have their backs."

Over the next several minutes, Vincent showed me around the office. We walked past several cubicles where folks were either preparing for lunch or still on calls. There were a good portion that Vincent did not recognize, but roughly one out of every five gave Vincent a look of shock and awe, a handshake or a hug, and shared stories.

There was Dotty, whom Vincent had hired but who never got to work for him despite her desire to. There was Kent Farmer, who had been a subpar rep but moved into an order-writer role and was loving it. There was Al Davidson, who was a pastor that enjoyed football. They talked briefly about the Vikings and 49ers.

These people treated Vincent like he was a returning war hero or celebrity. He handled it all very graciously, was complimentary of each of them and so genuine. It was evident Vincent enjoyed this; enjoyed being back in this office that saw the birth of a salesman.

The stories revealed a lot of the subsequent changes and brought up several old names.

Ted Benton – Vincent's college buddy – had left for advertising, came back for another tour and then left again for a technical role and then a government contract.

Jeff Mason had taken a role in advertising, then a promotion and wound up moving to Dallas and was now in the hospice care consultancy business.

Jane Daughtry had transferred to the center in Austin 12 years ago and was still there to this day.

100

Jay Zander had followed Vincent to advertising, then moved to Dallas in the finance organization.

Sadly, Cliff Marlin had been in an accident that was fatal to his passenger and he was on the slow mend.

They told him how great he looked, asked if he was coming back, and reminisced about memories from nearly two decades ago.

Finally, we saw Danny Nance. Danny was now a manager in the center. He had been hired in 2004, worked for Dick Knoll for a time and eventually worked for Vincent. He had been promoted to management after Vincent left the center and was still here over a decade later in the same role - just a bit more grizzled.

Nance was flanked by Chris Stills. Chris had started as a sales rep in Mankato, transferred to Minneapolis in 2004 and was promoted to management in 2008.

After we collectively met one another, our group walked across the street to Billy's Rockford for some quality pub food.

They picked Vincent's brain on how to better network, leverage their skills, promote themselves and put themselves into position for promotion. Both had been in role for a long time and were worried about the prospects of ABM Rockford; what would they do if the center shut down? Neither had spent a ton of time looking at how they could parlay their skills into other roles, either in the business or elsewhere.

Vincent had not seen them in a decade, nor had he been in this office for even longer. Danny and Chris had to return to work due to a strict hour-long, monitored lunch policy, but Vincent and I stayed, sipping on diet sodas.

"What was that like?" I asked.

"It was good. Surreal to walk through that place again. For so long, I felt like I couldn't go back in there. So, to have done it...to have seen all of those folks – it felt like closure. Much needed closure."

"It seemed like Danny and Chris were pumping you for info to help themselves, amidst all of the nostalgia. How did this lunch come together?"

"They asked me to lunch," he replied. "I told them I'd meet them at the office and would love to take a look around. That was the self-serving part. Everything these days is give-get."

I laughed.

"Why was that important to you?"

"I went through so much here and at ABM," Vincent replied slowly. "Those people – you saw them. They acted genuinely happy to see me and to celebrate a time we were all working together. That feeling – when it's gone, it's gone. When I got fired, I went from getting phone calls and requests – from needs – all the time to nothing. Complete silence. People wouldn't even talk to me or return my calls. They didn't care.

"You don't truly understand having been at the top until you're at the bottom."

"How did it feel to see these people today?"

"It's like stepping back in time. I mean, in some ways it feels like yesterday I worked there. You drive up, and you see these buildings or restaurants or even spots in the office that bring back so many memories – walking with a group of folks to lunch, team huddles in the middle of the floor. The reps and managers that worked in that building alongside me.

"In the same way, the whole thing haunts me. I am pretty good at focusing on the present moment, but it's always in the back of my mind – what could have been?"

"But you've far surpassed what you were doing then," I commented.

"In some ways, yes," he replied, not sounding sure of his response. "I felt like I was building and steering and the captain of the ship. I felt like I had a profound impact on these folks – mostly in a positive way. I so much enjoyed the science of it, figuring out the campaigns and the leads and moving us around, then tracking the stats.

"Financially, there's no question I've surpassed what I did. I just don't know sometimes if I'm making a difference. If I'm doing what I'm called to do."

"What do you think that is?"

"I'm still trying to figure that out. I just want to have as much of a positive impact on people as I can."

"Don't you mentor people?"

"Yes."

102

"And the podcasts you're on and articles you write – people contact you as a result, right?"

"Yes," he said.

"I dare say you're having more of an impact now on a global scale than you had once upon a time in a call center," I pointed out. "I get it – there are things you enjoyed about that gig. But sometimes you've got to infuse what you love into what you do."

Vincent laughed slightly, "Hey, look at you. Dropping some knowledge. Yeah, yeah, I know. The pity party's over.

"Sometimes I think it's all of the changes. I know I was ready to leave the ABM advertising role when I got fired. It had changed beyond the point of tolerance and growth. Doesn't mean I don't miss elements of it. It's like when a relationship ends – even one that's not good for you. You tend to glorify the good times.

"Terrifyingly, ABM was the steadiest thing I had ever had! Sure, I moved roles every couple of years, but I'd spend 5 years at a time with roughly the same folks. Since then, I bounced around every year or so until I got to Majestech-Ware. I've been in whatever this business is or has been for 6 years but I've had 7 managers and a title change every 6 months for the last 4 years.

"I loved working for Jeremy Rivers; he left January 2018 to join John Deever and Matt Rockwell at their startup vendor. The rest of my original team had already left for other roles. The turnover of the team, from either internal shift or departure was 100%.

"Sometimes I just felt really out of place and disliked, but members of my team acted blown away by my prospecting and my progress. I was having really good continuing conversations with Jordan Waters, who was highly regarded at CTMI and seemed to highly regard me. And when I got down – which was still at least once or twice a week – Jake Zuniga could typically give me an effective pep talk over a few drinks and pizza bread from the pub down the street from the office.

"For 2018, they changed our roles again; we had call center reps who started managing accounts in our territory. The call center was separate from the field. Fortunately, I had a good one – Kelly Docker. She was great – very self-sufficient. I never had a single issue with her. She communicated with me and kept me posted on everything in our mutual territory. Having her actually was a significant boost to the market. I needed it, since I was barely over 80% for the first half of our year.

"Janet Leary – my GM - did ask me to present at our kickoff – to the inside and field organization – on my prospecting and successes. That was nice. I definitely felt like I was headed in the right direction, but I didn't trust it and didn't have the numbers to back it up yet. I was still skeptical when people said positive things about me. Quintana – and, well, ABM long before her – had taken away any real faith I had that people I worked with actually liked me or respected me or valued me."

"That's tragic, and quite unsettling given the true impact you have had on those organizations," I said.

"The VP even reached out to me to hear what I was doing. I guess if I had to summarize – I never felt or feel secure. I feel like at any minute – especially here – somebody's going to realize I'm a fraud and get rid of me."

"Why do you feel like you're a fraud?"

"I'm not the prototypical seller for this environment."

"Which is the very reason you have been successful."

"True, but what if the luck runs out?"

"Has it yet?"

He laughed again. "Touché."

The waitress refilled our drinks, and we thanked her.

"I didn't understand everything that was going on in the inner workings of our product or the technical speak. But I did have a knack for leading the team and the meetings. I understood the high-level initiatives our customers and partners were doing well enough to express it to the team and dictate how things should move forward. And I was starting to get rave reviews from folks all over our business. Now, I just needed to hit goal.

"Those final six months of the fiscal year were a grind. There was just so much thankless, relentless back-and-forth tussling with customers and processes and utter nonsense.

"Case in point: I canceled the majority of my day once to sit in a full day session with a client – keep in mind, I had 200 at the time – while they were doing discovery with a partner, because I knew I could add value and show of support from CTMI. It made sense, I was kind of the ambassador of our business, and I opted to do it. That didn't cease my day job, though, and I had to IM folks to cover me for things, delegate tasks and reply to messages from time to time. Some lady in there who sat near me actually complained to the partner because I was doing business not affiliated with their organization and fretted that it was 'counter to their culture'. So, I had to basically apologize and explain it to the customer and partner after the fact.

"Another example – if I followed our funding processes *implicitly*, it was like pulling teeth to get any money for our customers. However, if I concocted a wonderful story about what was possible, hit the right talking points, and basically came hat in hand, throwing myself graciously out there for feedback and guidance, I got whatever I want. The governing body who granted funding was called the 'Deal Den.' I was on there a lot and so I got to the point I was a master of navigating those discussions. I eventually became known as the 'King of the Deal Den' because I went on quite a winning streak with them.

"They were tough on newcomers and certainly made you earn your bread, but once I learned how to negotiate and navigate these waters I was far more successful.

"However, getting the funding approval was one thing; once you had approval, there was a litany of other steps that had to be hit, administrative tasks undertaken and forms and agreements that had to be signed between every involved company. If we were paying a vendor to build a customization on top of our data platform, they'd have to produce a customized work statement, everyone would have to sign off on it; we had our own qualifiers for what we'd pay for and what we wouldn't, and there was a ton of back and forth and often milestones we'd hit would be ignored internally and we'd get threats funding would be pulled – even though we did everything right.

"We had to file forms to get any incentives, modify the forms if we needed to change any component of the deal, we had another form if we couldn't land certain 'strategic offerings' on the deal basically asking for forgiveness; and every time there was any error or perception of error, the whole process started over. Even for failed deals, I'd have to go through *all* of these steps just in the *chance* we could get a signed contract. So, I spent a lot of time managing the paper flow. I spent a lot of time chasing a lot of funding and incentives for deals that had to be drafted and redrafted multiple times, only to die on the table. It was time-consuming and exhausting. And mind-numbing.

"Fortunately, I continued to see Dr. Fleming – my therapist I started seeing years ago. Sometimes with Abby which was quite helpful. We – like many couples – had a lot of baggage and issues to work through and it brought us closer. But my biggest pains were from the time of ABM and the years since. The situation was remedied in the courts, but it didn't make it all go away. The trust issues, the trepidation with which I now ran my life – it never left. I had become a master of pushing all negativity and doubt and fear down under a virtual rug – but that eventually catches up to you.

"These deals, man. There was the agricultural company who kept saying they were going to do this large deal and it wound up closing for 5% of the original scope.

"You'd get whiffs that a partner thought we could land a large upsell at an account, only to talk to the customer yourself and realize the deal had no legs whatsoever – meaning the vendor was feeding you a line of nonsense.

"You'd spend countless hours talking to customers and vendors, believing you were working toward a deal only to have something unravel – a competitive threat, a licensing issue, a discounting issue because of licensing, funding dollars that didn't come through, the signor would be on vacation when the deal had to come in, or the partner dropped the ball and didn't do something on time or what they were told to do. Endless, countless frustrations.

"What I learned – unfortunately not in my first year with Quintana, but it served me well subsequently – is that half the battle was knowing how you could manipulate the licensing, merger and acquisition scenarios, funding, credits – all of the little nuances. So much else was an act of congress – getting buy-in and support from the business stakeholders, taking it to the board, awaiting approval or budget and then ultimately getting shot down. I had to augment natural results or results from net new or upsell sales motions with manipulation of licensing configurations.

"I had a deal at an airline. A partner out of California brought it to me. They would build a data and predictive maintenance model with a platform that would interact with all of their data sources. Fine and good. The partner was proposing to the customer they'd sell a month-to-month licensing structure and it would start when the project kicked off in October. Two problems with that: one –

106

if they sold that model, my team realizes one month of that revenue at a time, instead of 12 months upfront. Second – they would be buying in October and I'd get none of that money in this fiscal year. I needed it now.

"But you don't get a win unless the other players win, too. So, you have to create a scenario where everybody gets something they want – something that's attractive.

"Every deal has to have some give-get, and anyone who tells you differently doesn't know how to construct a deal. I find myself trying to offer price parity, positioning a deal that will maximize CTMI upfront revenue and at the same time include components that will help me when I sell the story internally."

"How so?" I inquired, fascinated.

"I know I can sell a deal internally, for discounting and funding, if I include certain add-on's, plus sell a vision of a roadmap. The 'what's possible' if we land this deal. Part of the deal is the internal politics. Sometimes, that's also staying off radars; I know I can secure $149K in any given funding bucket but not a dollar more without having to answer to a different governing body.

"The other side is the customer expectations. They know full well they can wait until October and pay month to month, and what that cost will look like this year, next year and over 10 years. So I have to make it worth their while, whether it's billing them upfront for a multi-year contract and then offering some type of payment solution where I eat their finance charges, all while tying in funding dollars they would not have gotten otherwise, or structuring the deal in a way that allows the optimum amounts of discounting and funding. Bottom line: The more money CTMI might realize in this fiscal year, the more likely I can extend discounting and funding dollars for the build-out of the proposed architecture.

"And I've found the best way to convey this to a customer is full transparency."

"What do you mean?"

"Pull back the curtain. Show them the wizard. You can't cram anything down their throats; they're too smart for that. But you can gain their trust by best playing your role as their advocate. My entire job is to utilize my knowledge of all of the programs and resources within CTMI to benefit them. Sure, I'll tell them that we're adding these additional bolt-on's, but I'll explain it's because we can extend more discounting and basically eat the cost. They don't care if the reason is because it's going to pay my team and me more. Additionally, I'll absolutely spell out that the more revenue we can realize in this period, the better deal I can concoct for them.

"They get what they want. In fact, I'll often deliver under price over a year, 3-year, 5-year, 10-year analysis on purpose. The company wins – because we realize more money upfront, we neutralize competitive threats because of the quality of the deal, and we lock in long-term. A month-to-month agreement with one of our vendors doesn't hold the same level of stability as a multi-year deal with CTMI."

"*Neutralize competitive threats* – I love that. I think that's one a lot of folks miss on with short-sightedness. But don't you worry about your metrics being jacked up next year as a result of selling this deal?"

"No, not at all," Vincent responded immediately. "I can't control what will happen next year. I may not be in the same job. I may not have the same territory. Any number of things can change. In sales, you optimize the now and focus on the customer's long-term while giving no thought whatsoever to your own tomorrow."

"Holy mackerel," I marveled. "So, this airline – you cooked up some magical deal and crushed goal?"

"That's half right," Vincent said, sipping his soda again. "I cooked up the deal. The CFO balked in the 11th hour and pushed it by a year because they were not ready to implement. They couldn't get the budget to overhaul their platform. Another heartbreaker. This job is full of them."

I shook my head. "And how much time did you spend on that?"

"Between all of the calls with the customer, calls with my team, planning, submitting for funding and discounts, having the partners draw up the necessary paperwork – I'd say I personally spent 11 hours on it, but the far greater impact is everyone else who touched it. But that's how the game works. You win some, you lose some and you learn lots.

"I spent countless hours coordinating and participating in a data solution for a streaming movie service. Lots of travel was involved, my team and I scoped a dozen partners who could build add-on's to the CTMI platform which would make this thing really hum for the organization. We got really deep into negotiation and I structured a very complex, lucrative deal that would be over 10 years. I got a call from their CEO with a few weeks left in the fiscal year and they went with a competitor."

"My gosh – why did they go elsewhere after all that? What did you do?"

"I didn't ask."

"*What?*" I said, a bit shocked.

"What difference did it make at that point? I already knew why. I had ceded too much control to the partners. It became convoluted. The more complex your deal, the easier for a customer to say no.

"We should have sold the platform on its merits for a smaller piece of the solution, the business fix. Then, perhaps tried to replace other components of their business as we collectively saw fit. Instead, we were trying to take on the world. And I didn't stop it. I thought it was truly viable.

"One thing after another, we kept collectively finding ways to tackle things they had identified as priorities in discovery and we just tacked them on. It became very bulky with a lot of hands on deck.

"But when a dozen other partners were in the mix, it was too much noise for the customer. And the competing solution did a lot of what they were looking to do out of the gate on their own timeline. It taught me that while team selling was imperative, my own control of the deal had to be supreme. I had to be single point of truth, running point on the deal and managing everyone's expectations and piece of the pie.

"It's hard because there is so much potential and possible vision. You have a great meeting with senior execs in an organization, and there are always countless initiatives on everyone's wish list. There's so much you can and could do together. But then the initial attraction wears a bit and you're back to reality – budgets, timelines, milestones, existing solutions, other priorities. It's a wonder we can ever sell anything."

"How do you come back from deals going sideways like that?"

"Again - what choice do I have? I have a family to support. I have a reputation to maintain. Or, at least, I did at one point. Now my reputation was murky anyway." Vincent laughed a bit, but it was an uncomfortable laugh.

"So those final six months of the year," he continued, "I'm being paraded around for my prospecting and pipeline generation prowess, all while I could not get the big deals closed. I felt like a fraud. Everything would be for naught if I couldn't muster much more than 80% to goal.

"My new boss knew it, too. David Anthony – he had been one of my peers previously under Jeremy Rivers – took the role in January 2018. It happened quickly enough that it was clearly orchestrated behind the scenes when Jeremy decided to leave. The nice thing is while Dave had been doing my current role for some time previously and had a lot of credible, worldly experience, he looked up to me for my unique skill set and deep leadership background. He told me more than anything he wanted to see me bring my burgeoning, strengthening brand of being the best prospector in the business to fruition via massive results. It would redeem me, but it would also show that my methods as the 'new type of seller this organization needed' were founded.

"I actually found that ironic, since I was pushing 40, trying to recapture what I had in my 20's and being called the 'new type of seller.'

"It didn't get any easier. A large hotel chain – I had all the right relationships, all of the compelling use cases. But they were a century old and old school family-owned and while I could sell the concept to anybody within the business, the CEO didn't want to change their ways of doing business. That could have been a million-dollar deal – everyone was sure to point that out to me. CTMI and the vendor – I guess – expected me to somehow wave a magic wand and get the deal done anyway."

"Don't you love the unrealistic expectations of people in sales?"

"Not even a little." We chuckled together.

He continued, "Even the deals I *was* landing took monumental effort and resulted in complete upheaval amongst the team, customers, and vendors. I had a mining company who got our platform for internal collaboration with their various sites. They had made a few acquisitions in recent years. Their holding company was sans agreement while the primary mining company was the only one with our product.

"So, I called in their vendor to construct a deal including all of the subsidiaries. This thing took massive amounts of time; our licensing didn't make it any easier. I had to personally go out and meet with the CEO a couple of times to stress why this was a good deal, even though on paper I understood some of his concerns. We were absolutely asking them to move up their intended deployment dates, and our licensing model actually required them to buy bundles containing some of the stuff they already owned; I extended a sizable discount – which took a lot of doing internally to secure – but they were confused and the vendor was doing us no favors with their incompetence in sizing and scoping this thing.

"We landed the deal, but in the aftermath, they felt like they got hosed because the vendor didn't come through on several of the promised action items. No matter how much it wasn't my fault, I was always at the front of the deal and I had to take it on the chin.

"There was a real positive coming out of all of this, though. I was getting a lot of notoriety with Janet Leary. I had to secure larger discounts from her, and she was obviously privy to my speaking tour on prospecting and the pipeline I was driving, my surveys, and other buzz I was getting from the field.

"Even though I had deals going belly-up, I was building more of them than anyone else – by far. She loved my creativity of how I was positioning deals, how I was structuring them and my thought process on strategy. I was willing to do whatever it took creatively and collaboratively, to construct and win a deal. And that earned me a lot of points and positive press.

"Additionally, Dave Anthony seemed very much to be in my corner. He even had me fly to Houston to interview candidates for his replacement. One of those candidates was an old friend of mine – Fred Hampton, who used to be my peer when I was a Regional Business Manager for Majestech-Ware. He got my vote, but he didn't get the gig. This round, anyway."

He winked, then continued.

"Perhaps one of the most noteworthy things for me and my family about 2018, though, was church. It was when we became members of our current church. Our kids were both baptized, which had been a major point of contention in years prior when Abby and I were not together. I've often said – faith, family and friends are everything. And I was finally figuring out what that really meant.

"I felt empty... feel empty in a lot of ways," Vincent said, sullenly. "I have to plug the gaps with faith, family and friends.

"I'm just doing what I know how to do – running sales campaigns and marketing events and webinars for our vendors, prospecting, having conversations, coming out with opportunities, attaching the right resource and then orchestrating. There's a lot of fallout, but if you can manage to get enough stuff to the goal line, you're good.

"I've never been in an environment where I felt relatively so little control, and I managed a three-state call center initiative. So many conversations... and you look back and a lot of them didn't matter at all. The major deals I got done, I really only had a make or break impact during certain phases of the deal or with certain deals – the rest was like a sporting event. I can make the lineup card, I can call the plays, but the game is played and we can only adjust and adapt as it goes on.

"Few if any of our vendors drive deals alone; it's constant driving, babysitting, and hand-holding.

"But I did get a call from my old GM Jordan Waters – he was hearing rave reviews of me. Janet Leary continued to have me speak to different districts about my strategies and how they were working. More and more people reached out for me to mentor them or go through my process. I was getting frequent praise, but I never felt comfortable.

"Even though my results were not where they wanted to be, I was doing a lot of public press and outreach on deals that involved many others. I was making new connections and making a name for myself in new ways.

"I'd also field inquiries internally, from our Large Business Group, from our hardware channel again, and even from vendors if I would be interested in joining their ranks. A change sounded enticing, but I wasn't in the mood to reboot, recreate, reconjure myself for yet another iteration; I was running on motivation from being condemned, and that's all that prevented burnout from taking over.

"My motivation was legendary once, but it slipped away. Not hitting numbers and having so many deals go awry after all the time and energy I spent, with little control to do much else was...not humbling, just annoying. It eroded my belief I could dominate this role as I have every role I've had. I suppose that's pompous, but it's true. I'm not used to failing.

"I had the deals lined up to hit my number, but they all fell flat or snagged or got pushed several months meaning they would fall into the following year.

"And then vendors would sell with their own self-interests; they made more margin on month-to-month direct deals rather than going through us on our paper. Some of our vendors would just sell those types of deals behind our back, without my knowledge or support. And it meant *major* hits to my team's and my performance versus quota. It also made my forecast look inaccurate. Quintana already had me skittish about that.

112

"This happened with two of my largest potential opportunities for the back half of the year. It made us look really stupid, because we appeared to have no idea what our vendors were doing with our own product in our own territory. We weren't on the same page. And it was yet another area where we and I lost control.

"So, things continued like that much of the first half of calendar 2018 – I did my routines, my workouts to stay sane, went to work and tried to pull together the chaos, and saw a lot of things collapse. Or never take flight.

"But I realized something. Because I was so good at creating a compelling event or manipulating the variables, I decided to start calling on every client with existing contracts and offering credits that would stay off the Deal Den's radar for them to commit to more product. Between then and June, I signed 14 upsells totaling $1.7 million.

"Furthermore, as time got closer to our end of fiscal, our coffers got a little more lucrative because we were more willing to make deals. I signed a couple of new agreements and one renewal where we struck significant new revenue and add-on's.

"Finally, there was a mid-size organization called Bill Process Management – or BPM – in St. Paul. They had always done a lot of business with our competitors with one segment of their business on our platform but managed their business units in a siloed fashion. They had a unit who managed payment processes and auditing for healthcare, government, education and other industry verticals, and had always managed these divisions distinctly. Well, one day they named a new CEO – Charles Royal – and I saw opportunity.

"After seeing the news flash on my LinkedIn and seeing it in the *Business Journal*, I messaged him via LinkedIn. Very respectfully - 'Hi, I lead the BPM-CTMI partnership and would love to see where I may best support your initiatives with resources you are entitled to, all while giving you the lowdown on the Twin Cities.' He was relocating from California to take this job.

"I got a response, and was in his office the following week, before any of our competitors.

"We hit it off straightaway. What I loved about Charles was he was very candid, very straightforward. He told me exactly what he did and didn't like about his provider and vendor relationships in the past. He asked me what I thought of my relationship up to this point with BPM, and I was honest in kind – that while I

113

had enjoyed chats with his VP Shane Madden, they rarely went far because the business was being managed so differently. I gently but directly questioned the siloed approach, considering surely they had data and insights that could be used across the enterprise.

"I'm not saying I was responsible, but Charles decided to manage his entire business as one – bringing the business units together and putting Shane in charge of them. But what I was *certainly* responsible for was getting in very quickly to forge the new relationship with Charles before any competitors could. Then, I moved to introduce him to internal and vendor resources that could help him realize his vision. He could holistically manage BPM and bring everyone onto the same platform so they could share data where it made sense and glean insights on a much larger data set. It would also enable them to explore new industry verticals and business offerings.

"It took some doing, but because of my relationship with Janet Leary, my GM, I was able to secure a very healthy discount to close a large June deal with BPM. I finished the year at 100.1% to goal. And I was absolutely exhausted."

He sat back for a moment, took a sip of water and was quiet.

Chapter 8 – Go West, Young Man

"So, you did it," I proclaimed. "Comeback complete?"

"Hardly," Vincent responded. "I left it all on the field but lost a ton of possible deals and barely hit the number despite having driven so much pipeline. I still felt like I was preaching pipeline practices while I couldn't close the big deals. Our role changed shortly thereafter – again – and most of the pipeline I had driven was given to another territory for parity purposes. They claimed it was geographical or opportunity-based realignment, but come on.

"I 'won' but I didn't beat it. The specter of defeat from Quintana was still very much alive and well in me. Dave Anthony kept telling me I needed to fully realize the fruits of my labor; get the payout that was possible and really figure out how to master the role. I was on the path, but I hadn't done it. And I didn't know if I had it in me at all to continue."

"Interesting," I acknowledged. "So, what did you do?"

"The only thing I know how to do – reflect that I'm OK, my family is OK. Take solace in the fact that I have everything I've ever wanted in my life. And take one step, one moment, one conversation at a time. Slow it down. And then I went hiking and climbing mountains in the wilderness in Washington back country for two weeks and thought I was going to die."

"*What?*" I exclaimed.

"Yeah," he responded, then he signaled to the door. "Ready to go?"

I insisted on picking up the tab. We took final sips of our drinks and departed, walking back across the lot to his car.

"Where to?" I inquired.

"One last important stop before I take you to the airport," he replied. "If you're going to write about me, it will complete the picture. You saw my first office, you saw my last office. I'll show you the rest of the story."

We got in the car and buckled. He checked the mirrors and we drove out of the lot.

"So - the back country?"

"Later," he said. "I'll show you the pictures."

"Fair enough," I accepted. "Let's get some more philosophy questions out there."

We got back onto I-55, heading east. It was a little after 2 PM in the afternoon; still sunny. Vincent had the top down on the convertible, and it was once again a wonderful drive through gorgeous Minneapolis suburbs. We eventually found our way to MN-100 South.

"You talk a lot about process," I continued. "Process being critical to building pipeline, forming relationships and driving toward the deal. What's that process look like after the deal is done? You've highlighted some relationships you cultivated. What does value look like after the sale?"

"I love it," responded Vincent right away. I could tell he was so in his element when he talked about his family and his love of coaching and the deal. He just sounded tired when he talked about his job. "Because that can be a big miss for a lot of sellers; the deal is made, and they just move on.

"I get it – sometimes our 'process' or lack thereof creates that problem. There's no implied incentive to camp out and see it through and any potential upsell isn't right around the corner, so we turn our focus elsewhere. But having part of your process be inclusive of these existing relationships is very important – from a referral *and* potential upsell perspective. Plus, your contacts may go elsewhere in the organization or to other companies, opening up a whole new potential relationship.

"Everything we do is about adding value and building relationships. It takes five seconds to message someone and tell them they matter and you appreciate them. Likewise, it takes just a moment to send a note over to a client just to check in. They'll honestly – and sadly – be surprised that you're reaching out just to gauge their well-being. I send notes at the holidays, too – telling them I'm thankful for the partnership at Thanksgiving and thanking them for the work we've done together during the year as Christmas vacation arrives.

"Ask them if they would benefit from a conversation – if there's anything you can be doing. Cut and paste it as a template if you're really looking to optimize your time and send it to a lot of people. The true impact is when it lands in their inbox and you stay top of mind, but you also come across as a true partner. That stuff resonates. That stuff matters.

116

"I have spent a lot of time focused on trying to bring value to my clients' existing investments. You start with their agenda of what matters most to them, and – of course – while you're there, you get the opportunity to bring up what matters to you, too.

"Ideally, you develop a relationship with a client where they care about your deal cycles and what gets you paid. In turn, you understand what their priorities are and what business problems they are trying to solve. You deliver value because you're paid to support that client with all of your existing programs and offerings they wouldn't know about otherwise. You can also support the relationships as a resource – to introduce them to others who can help or taking an outside the box approach to deliver value. Sometimes, there's not a fit. Sometimes there is, and magic is created.

"Ideally, planets align, and you create or come across an opportunity – for a partnership that will bear fruit. But, if you stick around, you'll be there again – this time as a trusted resource – to see more opportunity come about. Value after the sale is a meaningful presence.

"If we handle this balance properly, we'll always be hunting and farming. We'll have more to farm, but making time for hunting ensures there's no famine.

"Schedule time – maybe it's monthly, maybe it's quarterly – to make a touchpoint. It takes just seconds to message a client to see if it makes sense to get together or if they'd benefit from a conversation. Or if you see an article that harkens back to a previous conversation, to send it over to show you thought of what they said. Or you see their company in the news, or some type of merger and acquisition movement and wanted to gauge how it affects them and how you may be able to help amidst the change. Or you see on social it's their birthday. Unashamedly take every opportunity to make a quality touch. That's how you stand out. That's how you earn a special partnership they don't have with others.

"When your customers' or their businesses' needs change, if you're plugged in, you can often help them with those new needs. I've even gone so far as to help them get plugged in at a competitor, because I knew they needed or wanted the competing solution and I had a contact over there. Establish yourself as the go-to and the trusted advisor for everything you can. That stuff can take just a moment but it's another investment into a partnership that will pay a variety of dividends.

"Always prioritize based on the warmth of your 'leads' or relationships and the correlating magnitude of the work. Drop everything when one is directly talking to you in a meaningful way that gets you a step closer to where you want to go together. The warmest lead is one you've already won with.

"If you are consistent with your outreach and cadence and you find ways to make quality touches, you'll be top of mind and you'll have as best of a relationship with them as you can."

"How do you cut through all of the noise?" I asked. "When you get a lot of tasks or busy work or non-revenue generating activity from a customer or potential customer?"

"It definitely happens, doesn't it?" he mused. "When they are on your radar as a potential client and you want to move forward, but they're raising all of these red flags. Or complaints. Or they are tasking you with informing them for a considerable period without advancing in the buying mode. Dating without taking it to the next level in the relationship.

"Again, it comes to priorities, and – frankly – unashamedly managing your time. Always be respectful, but if you have clients that are taking up a preponderance of your time with activities and milestones that get you and your company paid, you have to manage your time in a way that those checkpoints get hit. That's what you're paid to do – to effectively manage your time in a way that realizes the results you're charged with getting. Call in help if you have to.

"On the same token, I absolutely believe you need to be available and answer the bell for the ones for whom you are either managing a relationship or the ones you are attempting to advance. Yes, you ensure you respond and act. Sometimes, you buy yourself time; use your out-of-office if you're in a session all-day with a client or you're traveling and it will impede your response time. I use an out of office that tells them what to do 'for the immediate response' they deserve.

"Set realistic expectations with these folks of what your time looks like, how you spend it, and engage other resources if you can to help answer questions or be available when you simply cannot be. It can be as simple as a quick e-mail reply from your phone adding in another or the proper contact – just to keep things moving.

"For me, it helps to remember and remind myself that my priorities have to center on what matters most...like faith – living my talents in the ways I am being called to do. My wife – am I providing, am I supporting? My kids. My friends. All of that bleeds into my work, because I'm a provider, and to effectively do work, you have to relegate 'the noise' to its rightful place.

"As I mentioned before, I took from Quintana how to aggressively manage my own schedule; push off things that don't have to happen today. And sometimes – often times - 'the noise' fits into that category. It doesn't have to be dealt with right away, and just because the client doesn't necessarily like the process for their concerns to be addressed, that doesn't always fall on you to fix.

"Customers take their investments – with you, or whomever – very seriously, so you should as well. Circle back to your principles – and theirs – when you are working with them on anything. Issues that they're having – they are rarely with you, unless you're not responsive. Even if you ask for time by acknowledging their request and saying you'll get back with them, you're present. You're there. They respect that more than lack of response, and more than you know. Because – sadly – it's rare to be as communicative as a customer desires. When you are, it makes a big difference. It stands out.

"It all boils down to communication – wherever you are in any step of any process. All situations benefit from communication and transparency."

"A lot of customers will allude to the fact you or your company is really present when you're in a sales cycle but otherwise the contact isn't as frequent. To be fair, if they are wanting to work together, they can signify that, too. But I always make it a point to tell clients that it's my role to show them not only new solutions, but how to optimize their existing investments. Frankly, that helps me get conversations scheduled with existing clients. The meeting originates because of their priorities, and then I can absolutely infuse the priorities of my company and me into an agenda.

"If you maintain a long-term relationship and prove yourself as a go-to resource, they will continue to reach out – and that won't always be with conversation that furthers the cause. Sometimes it will be 'noise' - like when they complain about something out of your control or they ask about something that really doesn't fall in your jurisdiction or they make a request that doesn't get you paid. But how you manage the noise will matter. Just don't let it overpower what you have to get done."

"Let's switch gears," I said. "You've told me before you write these books to outline the things you wish you had known earlier on. The lessons you've sometimes learned the hard way. What advice do you give a seller starting out?"

"Learn *everything*. And when I say that, I mean be humble and first learn when to speak and what to say. In my 20's, I got this sense I knew everything or knew best, and it wasn't until I started Majestech-Ware at 35 where I was truly coming in, accepting my role and limitations and just willing to be a contributor and learner. Fortunately, I've found even more success in this stage than when I thought I peaked. But knowing that you know relatively nothing in the grand scheme and the most important lessons aren't how to dominate your job but how to bend in change, adapt and evolve – these are things we don't know unless someone tells us.

"There's a lot of things we're not necessarily prepared for when we start our careers, or even get out of college or go to college. Elements of business, like playing politics, or how to react – or not react – when things happen that are unfair or you disagree with. Discipline. How to conduct yourself when things are not going the way you hoped or thought they would.

"I'd tell a seller starting out that you are going to pay a lot of dues. Likely far more than you really should have to, but that's just how it works. Like it or not, you're paid to follow company directive and be a custodian of that brand. As long as you accept their money, that's just how it goes. Act like it. If you have a forum to voice your concerns, do it respectfully but accept the laws of the land.

"Pay special mind to how you conduct yourself – on and off the field. If you become a liability, it's in their best interests to cut ties. We all have bad days, but you can control certain things and controlling the controllables and functioning without constantly looking for excuses for why you're not performing or doing what's expected will only serve to keep your stock from decreasing.

"That's the tough love stuff. I felt compelled to get it out there first because I take it so seriously and that's what I needed to hear when I was there. But *have fun*. Take the time to invest in *real* relationships. I still talk to people I worked with two decades ago. Far more than I talk to anyone in my graduating high school class. And nearly every gig I've ever been in transpired because of a relationship.

"Do your absolute best. Sometimes you have to slow it down to focus solely on the moment – taking the step you have to take to the clients' door or picking up the phone and just dialing – to silence or ignore or deal with the doubt you have in your mind. Other times will be so fast paced you'll blink and you miss it. But the thing you can control most is you – your effort. Are you doing the things that can and will lead to the result? Is the result next to your name indicative of your skill and effort? If it's not, what the heck are you doing?

"When inevitable storms hit your life and career, keep a consistent hand on the wheel and a cool head – these are times you have to slow it down and focus on process and people, not emotion.

"And be open to where they journey takes you. I had absolutely no idea what to expect of my career. I looked at it so differently at 20 when it was all ahead, and there were absolutely times where I wondered why things happened or what it was leading me toward. Take opportunities, take risks. Don't gamble with anything you're afraid to lose, but you'll never make a big gain without some strategic risks. Invest in people and in your network. Take advantage of every opportunity you can to learn – from people and from your organization.

"Most of all, infuse what you're passionate about into your job and career. You'll have some jobs you love passionately. You may have others you dislike. But bring your own one-of-a-kind talents to your job in a way that it keeps you going, makes you stand out, makes you invaluable. Find your place and then help others achieve more. Be selfless. Be mindful. No matter what you master or think you mastered, you'll always have a lot to learn. Approach everything with that mindset."

"Powerful stuff, my friend," I marveled. "As you pointed out, you've been doing this for over two decades. Compare and contrast – your early days selling to what you see in the sales world now. You've worked at big companies and small in myriad industries, for likely dozens of bosses. What's changed?"

Vincent laughed a bit. "Yeah, it's been quite some time. It's nice knowing I hopefully have a long way to go. It's been a sometimes fun, often wild ride to be certain. Starting out, I did the call center thing which is very different from what I do now in field sales. I've been in environments dialing the phone manually using spreadsheets and stick tallies to track outreach. Now, pretty much everything is governed by data, by automated processes and smart technology that scores leads and tells us propensity to buy."

"Is it better that way?"

"Sure, in some ways," Vincent reflected. "The value of the true seller has changed in that equation. The person who could sniff out opportunity, create and cultivate relationships and build a book of business and reputation looked a lot different twenty years ago. Now, there's so many more tools – you can find anyone on the Internet, find out everything about them, and keep in touch so easily. But I think that raises the bar. Because it is so easy to connect and find people, we have to find new ways to elevate the caliber of relationships.

"I don't care how much you can automate, or how easy it is to connect, it will never replace the value of the face-to-face in person meeting. The handshake. Looking them in the eyes across the table as you personally, passionately negotiate the deal.

"Everywhere a customer can be touched or reached, a sales opportunity exists. That landscape just looks a lot different now. It's broader. The needs and expectations are different. Nowadays, that instant gratification and immediate impulse is the norm, meaning delivery of the result has to happen at breakneck speed. So, as a seller, you now must be swift in delivery of expectations.

"We're also overly connected. When I started in sales, I had a landline phone in my apartment, dial-up Internet and a rarely used cellular phone because it had limitations on minutes and usage. There were no apps. Your hit-or-miss Internet connection featured messenger services where you could chat with people. Now, everything is the highest of speeds of communication. I'm connected all the time. My phone buzzes every few seconds from a work e-mail or social site, or my work messenger where someone can reach me every second of every day. We're more connected – which makes it all the more important to know when and how to disconnect."

"You went into the woods," I proffered, with a wry smile.

Vincent chuckled. "That again. Yeah, I promise we'll get there soon. But I think the biggest change I've seen in sales is what I thought I knew. I got a taste early on, did well, and thought I knew a fair amount. The more time that goes by, I realize I knew relatively nothing back then. But the things that matter – the personal touches – matter *more* in this age of technology. Because they are becoming less commonplace. Accounts are managed half a world away, rather than by someone who visits you regularly. You talk to a bot instead of a human. These things can be great if they lead to more coverage and better experience, but that isn't always the case. That onus falls on the company – to keep humans at the heart of their operation and their delivery."

122

"What's changed the most in your sales approach?"

"Becoming a *real* team player as opposed to just someone on a team," he said with no hesitation. "Sure, I was always on teams. But I started as an individual contributor and was in competition with others. Absolutely, I shared best practices, but really only to gain notoriety for myself. It was that ego-driven, twentysomething thing.

"When I was a manager, I was competing again, and always felt like everyone was out to get me. I wasn't as collaborative as I could have been or should have been. I always had the perspective that I had to be the best and I didn't need anything from the other members of the team; sure, I'd pick up on a best practice someone else was doing and I'd assimilate it into my arsenal. But I always felt like it was me against the world. Always.

"It truthfully wasn't until after I was broken and humbled multiple times that my viewpoint changed in that regard. I've told you I came into Majestech-Ware content to be a 'sixth-man' - I needed a job! A job I was promised - a 'done deal' I was told – fell through. I didn't feel like what I was coming into was a complete fit, and I was overwhelmed and challenged daily like I had never been before. The younger me couldn't have handled it – heck, I considered leaving ABM many times in those early days before I became the top rep and manager in their history. But the experience and discipline of having pushed through uncertainty and storms before got me through again.

"And I did it by relying on others, not being afraid to ask for answers or help or guidance or feedback. And now, I do it daily - I come, hat in hand, to ask for feedback and guidance and thoughts. I 'gain consensus' - that was another thing I was told by managers I didn't do years ago. There was a lot of truth in the feedback I got in my younger days – I just didn't want to hear it. And it all centered on how I worked with others.

"I thought sales excellence was all about being an excellent seller, but that's such a small part of the puzzle," Vincent explained. "Sales excellence is about being a student. Knowing the players, the parameters, the playing field – all of the little idiosyncrasies, like where and when to hit a bloop single on a baseball diamond instead of swinging for the fences, knowing your probabilities – those are the variables that drive true sales excellence. How to construct a compelling deal where *everybody* wins. How to best leverage the strengths of your entire team. Who to call in for any given scenario.

"I have known relatively little compared to my teams in years past of the technical aspects of the telecom business, the Internet business, the advertising business, the technology business. But I knew how to build a community around the product or service and my teams, how to prospect, drive awareness, make quality touches. I could do those things and leverage the smart people to help me get the deals done. That team component was missing from my early career. And that's why I've far eclipsed the success I once had.

"That team mentality expands the holy sales trinity," he continued, making hand gestures with his free right hand as the left remained on the steering wheel of the Aston Martin. "Because then it's not just about your company and you – there are other internal or partner or vendor elements at stake. The company component has another layer. Everybody has to win.

"I've made a concerted effort when anyone else is involved in a deal to proactively ascertain their feedback, even if I didn't really intend on using it initially. Because others who have a horse in the race or a relationship with your company and the customer may need to weigh in or be supportive of the deal. Bring them into the fold.

"This has helped tremendously if a vendor had a relationship with the customer and I had a potentially lesser relationship with the same customer; I need the vendor to help me. But why would they do that, especially if they thought my interests were different? I've frequently created some element of the deal solely so it would benefit the vendor I'm using to help me broker the dialogue or use as intermediary. It may not have been my preferred method, but if you have to utilize a proxy to sidle up to your target, so be it. Meet them where and how they want to be met. Involve them and engage them. Include them in the plan.

"I've watched the opposite approach; I've worked with sales reps who have tried to bring up other vendors or solutions with a vendor or partner on the phone or in the room! You're creating an unnecessary situation where one potential component of the relationship or deal is now against you. Even if it's not the best partner for the job, get their buy-in and earn them as an ally. You're better off for it. Let the customer remove that partner but don't do it yourself. You cannot do anything unilaterally or arbitrarily when another relationship exists in the equation.

"Be aware of every other player or potential player on your playing field and how your play impacts them. A time will come when their play impacts you.

"I make a point to win the crowd – something, ironically, a manager at Tel-Cell Wireless who didn't teach me much else told me several years ago. The line from *Gladiator*. There's no sense in being territorial. Everybody has a stake in these customers. I always make it a point to refer to customers as 'our mutual customers' when I'm talking to anyone internally, any other vendor, any partner – because it's true. They look at them like their customers, whether we're fighting the same fight or have slightly differing priorities. Talking to them like you own the place or run the show is just going to turn them off. Then, why would they help you?

"I tell every partner or potential partner 'I'm interested in whatever I can do to support your efforts,' because – fortunately – often if they win, I win too because my team's solution is tied in to what they are ultimately doing after customizations. I just have to facilitate the foundation or provide an environment conducive for mutually beneficial partnerships.

"Furthermore, these accounts are on loan. Nobody owns them. A rare seller covers an account or more for years upon years at a time; the vast majority change hands every few years. Frankly, that really benefits the sellers who have the ability to touch accounts for longer periods of time because they build trust. It also means we have to approach our interactions with these clients as collaborative instead of territorial."

"'On loan'," I contemplated for a moment. "You have a brilliant perspective. You're so right. Some people get so territorial about these accounts and their relationships to the point they try to box everyone else out, and while the relationships are important, why wouldn't you want organized team efforts in all of your accounts?"

"Agreed," Vincent said, switching lanes. "I understand wanting to keep folks at arm's length when it's haphazard outreach the seller isn't aware of, but provided it's collaborative and communication takes place, the more the merrier. Personally, I welcome an army of sellers driving results when I'm the one getting paid."

We were going south on I-494 toward MN-62. It was mid-afternoon and the sun's position indicated a few hours still of daylight.

"I guess that's where my head was heading into July 2018 and our fiscal year 2019," Vincent continued. "I lost 16 of my top accounts to Large Business Group or to re-mapping geographically. They said it was to offer parity opportunity-wise, but it was hogwash. 13 of my top deals for the coming year now belonged to someone else. So, I understand the inclination toward being territorial.

"On the flip side, there was quota I didn't have to worry about for the year. The accounts and deals were gone, but they were no longer factored into my quotas. It would be critical to figure out where I could best make my mark; which of my payout buckets I could best target and exploit. That's the real trick.

"Earlier that year, my father-in-law, Dan Winters, and brother-in-law Jamie, planned a backpacking trip to Rainier and the Cascades. It came up at my kids' baptism. I was like, 'sure, yeah, I'd consider it' but wasn't really all that serious. You know how when things come up and they are 7 months in the future, they seem lightyears away? I figured it would never come to fruition.

"But they kept talking about it. And Dan is a consummate planner. He absolutely started putting this whole trip together.

"Abby was supportive and the exhaustion from work and always being connected to work made me feel like, what the heck? Why not? I'd say, 'what's the worst that could happen' but we both know what that could have been.

"Dan was thrilled I was going. He took me out to help me buy all the stuff I'd need; some of it I thought I'd never use, but I used practically everything. Tent, mattress, rain gear, the pack, the water contraptions, cooking materials, freeze-dried food – you name it. The clothes, the Indiana Jones fedora and a shirt that looked like his, too. The walking poles. Headlamps. And – the most brilliant of all – a bottle to take a whiz in in the middle of the night so you don't have to go out in the dark with the wildlife."

I laughed.

"It could not have been timelier. I got my new territory assignment, received quota information, learned of my drastically impacted pipeline. Processes changed. People changed. Titles changed. The usual 'new year' rituals. It was time for me to go off the grid and check out completely. Get my head right. And feed my soul a little, too.

"The hardest thing is leaving the wife and kids for a couple of weeks, but in hindsight it was the best thing that could have happened to me at that point.

126

"We went with Robert Earley, a hiking friend of Dan's. He was more the spiritual and in-touch with nature kind of guy. Dan was the pacesetter who was a camping and hiking expert. Jamie and I were just there to experience it; he had gone out with these guys in the past at the Grand Tetons. This was my first rodeo.

"We spent a day just bumming around in Seattle. I turned off my work apps, so I couldn't be reached by the company – which is rare for me. We took in some local color; I had been there before a few times when my dear friend Jack Johnson was stationed in Everett with the Navy. We had lunch at Pike's Place and browsed the market. The seafood was excellent. The beer was excellent.

"We stayed at a cheap hotel and sipped booze out of paper cups. The next day, we loaded up on breakfast at Denny's and drove to Sunrise Camp – the highest point of Rainier you can reach with a vehicle.

"We got suited and sun-screened up. I had a 40-pound pack on my back – the first time I had done any real hiking or camping since Boy Scouts as a teenager. And, believe me, a lot has clearly changed in hiking and camping in the decades since then!

"The going was pretty good. Fortunately, Jamie and Rob needed more stops than Dan or me, so I got a break every so often. I was perfectly fine going uphill – in fact, I preferred it. The views were just unbelievable. You look at this majesty of nature and what God created and it's breathtaking. Surreal."

"How was it for the soul?" I asked. "I read an article the other day along the lines of 'Stressed? Need a Break? Take a Hike'."

"Spot on," he responded. "The formation was Dan on point – typically – then Jamie, then me, then Robert. We had a ton of inside jokes throughout the trip. Robert truly reminded me of my close friend Jack Johnson, but mid-50's. Jack had gone off to Yellowstone one summer when we were in college and returned a Buddhist with long hair wearing tie-dye. He was always good for a philosophical conversation over coffee. Robert was talking about the lion being his spirit animal, talking about the energy and lifeforce and would bask in the views we had and take in everything. He does yoga, he writes, he does music – *so* Jack. He kept the trip really tempered and reminded us to acknowledge our surroundings fully.

"He nicknamed me Tentacle. I told him a lot about my life, frankly because I felt this connection but also because we were by each other for two weeks straight. He could tell I was searching, but willing to reach out for different paths or relationships and open to new experiences. Spread my tentacles as it were. I liked it, too, since there are James Bond references to the octopus and it's the emblem of the crime organization in the books.

"He was so right. Frankly, since 2015, I had been *desperate* to *live*. To have new experiences. Travel more, as it made sense. Write. Just do new things. This definitely fell in line with that plight.

"I got pretty adept at assembling and dis-assembling my tent. Making the meals was actually really enjoyable; we had purchased little MSR Isopro fuel stoves, with various pots and containers. I took a liking to the pad Thai and curry. There was even this chocolate cake thing Dan brought that was a major hit. For breakfasts, I don't eat oatmeal in everyday life, but it was the most delicious thing ever after a night in the woods.

"I had the most incredible views for eating... and even for using the toilet...as I have ever had in my life."

I laughed again. Vincent was animated again, signaling to me that this was another fond memory.

"We spent a few nights out on each jaunt, hiking by day, finding camp and then cooking dinner. I'd breakfast on oatmeal, lunch on peanut butter and bagels. We'd snack on Kind bars and nuts, jerky, and dark chocolate. We had these Katadyn BeFree water bottles, so you could literally find any water source and drink from it thanks to the filters – there's nothing like going up to a steady stream or waterfall and being able to drink directly from it. And then we'd cook up a dinner at night.

"Rainier was basically just scenic for us; relatively easy hikes that we went on, only really touching on the base camp where climbers start their ascent on our last day.

"After that, we spent another night in Seattle, and the next day went to Marblemount – a small town a couple of hours from North Cascades. It was really the closest location to where we could start our entry. Half the fun was hanging out in these small towns, eating like kings because we were burning thousands of calories per day while out there and the rustic-looking hotel and restaurants.

"The Cascades – for me – was even more beautiful but more treacherous. I hated the unsure footing crossing snow fields or the tight trails where the drop-off literally immediately next to you was immense. I remember at one point we had to cross a chasm – there was nearly no way to go straight across. There was a literally

128

vertical column of rocks with water pouring from above. And there was an even more suspect 'walkway' above the water, but you'd have to climb vertically up the grassy embankment to get there.

"Well, that's the way Robert went. We all thought he was nuts. But he was the smallest of it and he pulled it off. Dan hopped horizontally across the chasm and grabbed onto the other side, pulling himself up. I was next. Come to find out, some guy was helivaced out just prior to our passing through for going that same way. I leapt across as best I could, and literally grabbed on to a brush of vegetation – clinging to it for dear life lest I'd slip down the side of this massive drop-off. I was pretty hesitant and nervous. But I felt like I was Indiana Jones. It was a bit exhilarating."

"Oh my gosh!" I exclaimed. "Insane! I can't even imagine!"

"Yeah, I had come a long way from home for sure," he continued. "But the trip taught me several things. I learned to have tunnel vision and just land each step. I slowed it down to the point that was my only priority – landing one step; I couldn't look around. I couldn't look where we were going or even where I had come from, or it would have scared the heck out of me. I looked at the step I had to land and put my energy into landing it. Didn't think about anything other than that.

"When it was time to rest, I'd rest. When we ate, I ate. But when we were out there hiking, and I was encountering unsure footing or grabbing on to whatever I could to keep from falling, I focused solely on that moment, that step, that security. It was all I could do.

"Pelton Basin was gorgeous. The view at our water source was incredible – we camped not far away. Looking up the face of the mountains it was like an Omnimax screen. The bugs were absolutely awful as we got any kind of altitude.

"I missed my girls something extremely fierce – and I would keep seeing things that reminded me of them. Sydney loved butterflies and I saw just one the whole time I was out there – a solitary butterfly. I took a video of it for her. Elizabeth loved these flaming hot Takis snacks – I saw some had been left behind in a bear cannister. There was a 16-mile hike day up and down parts of Sahale Mountain where at one point I stood on rocks, having stumbled a couple of times and just screamed an obscenity because I truly thought I had reached my limit. I thought I may fall. I thought I may die.

"Once, I had to climb up through a waterfall pouring down on me, getting foothold on and grabbing rocks where some moved and were unsteady and others weren't - like a death-defying Jenga game.

"It's interesting when - as much as I exercise, as much tolerance I have of stress and being pushed to my limits in life and career – this was like nothing I had ever experienced.

"When we got back to Marblemount – which, hilariously was a 2-hour drive from the Cascades *after* that tumultuous, exhausting 16-mile mountain hike – every single part of my body hurt in an intense way. *But my soul was on fire.* I had truly experienced a brand-new facet of life for me. And I wanted nothing more than to return to my girls and return and dominate my work."

"That's powerful," I stated, wrapping my head around the enormity of what he had said. The man with the unflappable confidence and drive had been flapped, and unplugging and pushing his physical self to the limits with a completely outside-the-comfort-zone experience had healed him. "Any key learnings?"

"Land the step. Just focus on landing the step – whatever that looks like for you. Close everything else out of your mind and slow it down to that level, specifically in times you're overwhelmed or just have to accomplish an individual milestone. It makes everything more digestible. A day achieved is an achievement in itself, and a day is just a series of steps.

"There's always so much noise, but out there it was just me and the land. The reality is we are surrounded by noise – some that's a part of our daily lives and jobs, but some we add ourselves. The news we follow, social media, what politics has become – these things can tug us in a million different directions. But we have to escape from all of that sometimes and focus on ourselves – our goals, our steps.

"No matter who you are, you have to unplug. I know my 50% of capacity may be better than a lot of people's and certainly better than nothing, but an experience that stimulates other senses and emotions and makes you appreciate everything you've got will get you to 100% - why *wouldn't* you want that? It's good for the soul.

"Also - never poop or eat where you sleep. The bears will get you."

We both chuckled heartily at this one.

"Just be open to experiences and opportunities. It's all an investment in your perspective, and your perspective becomes more valuable. I continue to be impressed by folks I meet who have traveled the world and know loads about different cultures. Before I was married with kids, I was married to my job. We've tried to make a concerted effort for more and new experiences."

"Well said," I reflected. "So, you came back, having lost all of those accounts and that pipeline. What was the lay of the land?"

"Yeah, I had lost 16 accounts – some pretty significant pipeline and some good relationships. Truth is, I could have fought for a few of them to keep. But I had done that the year before and it didn't turn out being worth it, so I let it lie. With 16 accounts and large pipeline, a lot of quota vanished as well, and I took a look at where I could make the biggest impact. It was on my public cloud component – hosting our solution in the cloud as opposed to on a server – and on our customized apps add-on.

"Having my edge back made it easier dealing with all of the changes. Our organization had turned into quite a circus, between the inside sales folks that were CTMI proper and the field sales folks who were legacy Majestech-Ware. Too many egos in the equation.

"The inside sales leadership was telling their teams they owned these accounts and to take *complete* control, almost treating us field folks like an anomaly. Like a subordinate. Fortunately, I had exceptionally strong client and partner relationships in the territory, so I had little to worry about. They needed me. I still had an all-up number to hit across all our products, so I could do pretty much whatever I wanted.

"I also had to work with all brand-new reps and specialists after they re-aligned territories. Our customers' biggest beef with us is the revolving door of support teams – they can't keep them straight. I was now aligned to a girl named Avery and a guy named Justin for the majority of the accounts; a few others were aligned here and there for a handful of them depending on industry vertical.

"While we lost a lot of the good prospects, we always get back the accounts Large Business Group doesn't want. Truly the minor leagues. The real bright spot is that they typically come back feeling unloved, having obviously not purchased anything over the last year. Every once in a while, you catch one in a cycle ready to buy. I didn't really see that happening, though, in this year's crop. We got a construction company, hospital and retail organization while Large Business Group got paid on my TGI deal. *Big time.*

"But – again – focus on the positive, drown out the negative. My quota was down. Control what I can control. Day at a time.

"I know from experience to construct my foundation – the master spreadsheet outlining every account, what they own, which vendors are involved, contract numbers and information on expiration – and then I create a separate field where I outline any opportunities for upsell or new products. I'll highlight where I see priorities. Especially when you have 100-to-200 accounts, it's important to determine your top 20 or 30.

"But I go down that list *every single day* from top to bottom, asking myself if there is anything I need to do on each account – be it a note to someone at the customer organization, be it some type of internal orchestration, nudging a vendor, you name it. And it works. It makes sure nothing is missed, and that the administrative tasks, e-mails and minutiae don't take you away from what will truly drive the business forward.

"The beginning of the fiscal year is travel time. We did the conference circuit. First, it's the big one, with the global draw; they hold it in Vegas. I always enjoy running into people I started with in 2014 that are still around. Now, because of my social platform and status everybody knows *me* there, which is quite surreal.

"Sometimes, you also wind up spending more time with folks that are closer to home that you don't see every day. In the airport back to Minneapolis, I ran into Jake Zuniga and Martin Shay, our most senior and longest tenured colleague in Minneapolis. He started at Majestech-Ware in 1985 when they were founded. He was employee 11. He had already had a few Crown and Coke's at the airport bar when we ran into him, and he insisted on buying us one after another as well. I didn't really want to drink on the flight home because I hate having to use the airplane bathroom, but this was one of those situations where you just do what you're told.

"He was telling us stories of the old days at Majestech-Ware, when the business was simple. Before it became the behemoth. When he had direct access regularly to the CEO and other senior leadership. Certainly, becoming a large organization doesn't happen without losing some of that feel, and the business model overall was working. Martin was really just a guy who wanted to take care of

132

his family and retreat to his 80-acres of hunting land in Kanabec County. The company had been good to him. Frankly, that is what I thought I would become for ABM.

"It was refreshing to hear that tale from a man who had spent 33 years with this same organization – since its inception. He had never sold a dime of his stock. He had his priorities in order.

"The travel circuit was actually much needed – to see that you're part of a larger organization with a lot of great things going on. The contributions we were making in health or in safety or in how people purchase goods and services they need daily – that was pretty cool. On top of that, there were so many great people. And the longer I've been there, the more of them I know and recognize and enjoy seeing when I'm doing the road show.

"Team offsites have always been enjoyable for me as well. I really gravitated toward the team I was on in 2018. Plus, they were typically in Dallas and I'd see my pal Jeff Mason. Those nights were always good for food, drink and bad karaoke.

"Finally, in September, we have a full United States seller session including all of the vendors.

"Going into that session was interesting, because during August – after I got back from Washington – I was asked by Janet Leary to helm multiple social selling and prospecting presentations again. The problem was I was known for this social selling stuff everybody thought made sense, but I had yet to have a breakout year so people didn't make the correlation that it could lead to stellar results. But it at least put me on a lot of radars; they knew who I was whether they thought I was worth listening to or thought my 15 minutes of fame here should be over.

"I did have some key wins – like FitSmart and BPM – that had only transpired because of social selling, and because results are all salespeople care about, I'd always lean heavily on presenting the nuts and bolts of how those deals came to be.

"It was also typically by the end of the first quarter of a new fiscal year that a lot of level promotions were made in the organization – more money, more stock, new title even in the same job. Since Quintana had clearly messed me over, since the role I took to enter Majestech-Ware didn't have a comparable level at CTMI, and since many of my peers were higher than I was in level despite my credentials – specifically from ABM, the books, the podcasts, etc., my new boss David Anthony seemed confident I'd be one of the ones to get a promotion. I was pretty happy about this. However, I found out night 1 of the seller-vendor conference that I wasn't getting one. The stink of Quintana was still apparently on me.

"But - at this conference – I was like the belle of the ball. People all knew me from these presentations I had been doing, my social media presence and ranking as the #1 social seller in the entire company so everyone wanted to connect.

"And vendors were making a play for me in droves, amidst the burn of being shunned for the promotion I was expecting. ABG was making another strong play for me; Nick Aragon was trying hard to convince me to give them another look. He assured me that managing partner Darren Miller and senior partner Shawn Wiseman would move mountains to get me. Apparently there was another new role working for Stefan Adams in Large Business Group and based on my bounce-back year and positive press they wanted me to interview; heck, the unmanaged patch was mostly the ones they took from my territory so it made logical sense.

"I can't even express the difference it makes when you go from feeling like this company is trying to eliminate you to a year later when everyone is making a play for you. People look at you differently, talk to you differently. There is a security and a strength. But having been where I'd been, I could handle it gracefully.

"So practically every conversation I had with a vendor or with colleagues seemed to carry undertones during the conference; I ran into Mick Logan, who introduced me to his boss Damian West and they were bending my ear about coming on board to focus solely on a new type of direct contract they were developing. These conversations could happen at the speed of cocktails because everybody was there.

"Truly everybody. I even ran into Quintana in-between learning sessions, and she hugged me. She – I guess – pretended to like me while we were surrounded by five thousand of our closest friends. A couple of people even walked by while we were chatting and knew who I was and commended me on everything I had been doing."

"I've noticed there's a lot of poetic justice in your life," I commented. "You always seem to run into these people who wronged you or with whom you have history."

"Yes, this is true. I've given that thought. I mean, I suppose the odds are pretty good you'll eventually cross paths with folks if you live in the same town, work in a similar industry or especially at the same company. But I have certainly managed to run into a few that I didn't expect.

"The benefit to having a lot of these folks know of me was that I was learning about openings on the applications sales team, an opening on the devices team and multiple vendor opportunities plus the Large Business Group interest. I struggled mightily with the fact that I wasn't getting the promotion I deserved that I was led to believe I'd be getting – and I quietly decided that it was time to leave one way or another. My stock was high, and if I didn't parlay that into something better given ample opportunity to do so, I was a fool if I didn't capitalize. What was going up could most certainly come down.

"But I still had to put one foot in front of the other. I've had an interesting career contrast; once a major player at ABM, but I had no personal brand or network. This go-around, my personal brand had thus far transcended my results. I had to get to a place where extreme results could be driven from the actions. But I also wanted to be somewhere I would be appreciated and make the money I deserved.

"That fall, I don't know what it was exactly, but our pastor was really delivering sermons where I thought every one of them was meant for me and only me. The most poignant was one about Philippians Chapter 4:11-13 - 'I receive my strength from the Lord.'

"The sermon was about how we go through these significant losses and if we cannot take any more and we're vulnerable and feel weak, then that verse is for us. I teared up and could barely breathe, looking at my own life. ABM *crushed* me, and Majestech-Ware and CTMI had made me feel really unwelcome – even changing rules to keep me down. I just couldn't get ahead. Couldn't get my just due. But the suffering and setbacks pale in comparison when I think about how good I truly do have it.

"It was actually during that time that the President of our CTMI U.S. division – Kelly Jergenson – reached out and interviewed me on her podcast about my process and prospecting. That one event was when recognition of me had a hockey stick spike. I thought I was known before in the company – this took it to a whole new level.

"This furthered my belief that I had no choice but to turn this momentum into something better for myself. Something actually befitting my skill level.

Dropping a hint to a few key people I know internally and at some of these vendor organizations that I was open to opportunities quickly led to a lot of interesting conversations. But I kept coming back to the ABG situation. I needed to find a way to get them to show me the money."

"What appealed to you?"

"The entrepreneurial side. The fact these guys actually really wanted me. The fact I could pretty much do whatever I wanted. My joy comes from doing more than the role typically entails, weaving in marketing and prospecting and then training others. They would have given me the reins on driving events and webinars and training sales, albeit to a much smaller team. Freedom. No constraints.

"But I had to play it smart. I just wanted to utilize my rising status to get what I deserved – even if it was just the promotion I deserved.

"Because I had propelled myself into a safer, valued status and had a good relationship with my boss, I *told* Dave Anthony *exactly* what was transpiring and that these various folks wanted me to apply for roles. To his credit, he was pretty supportive; even asked me to compile a wish list of what I wanted from my current role and division at CTMI. I appreciated that.

"It was never that I was trying to leave. Not at all. I always like to call it 'passively looking.' If something arises and there is a prospect it could be an improvement, take a conversation. See it through. Until you have a real decision to make, there's no action required on your part – just see where the process goes. And if and when an offer comes, you thoroughly weight out every variable in the equation. But, at this point, I was just trying to ascertain my worth and if what I wanted to do existed.

"I guess I could never figure out why CTMI wouldn't create a role for what I was so good at. At the seller-vendor conference, there were seminars you could go to. I signed up for one about 'How to target and pitch to the BDM, and construct and win complex deals' and it was a panel whose advice boiled down to really little more than 'use LinkedIn.' I could have trained that session and had the audience deliver a standing ovation. Instead, it was lackluster.

"I knew I could drive up everyone's results they'd allow me to touch, but they weren't thinking that way. They would certainly let me preach my best practices and stretch my role, but I wasn't worth promoting or paying for it. I struggled with the fact I was not asked to formally teach and coach and train this. Social selling was looked at as some kind of novelty. Like, they saw how it could help, and they talked about how important it was to break out of just working with IT, but when someone came along who could truly do it and do it better than anyone else, nothing was done about it. Everyone just kept humming along at status quo.

"I struggled, too, with the memory of ABM and how I felt when I was at the top of the mountain there; I've never felt that way again career-wise. And, personally, I struggled with the fact that for so long, I was my own only safe space. That's why I retreated when things went amiss outside of my control.

"I trained myself to need no one and trust no one because everyone had let me down. I rarely let myself feel anything. I could shut my emotions off in an instant. Those 1,229 days after ABM when I was completely alone with only my kid half the time as solace, while only a couple of people would even give me the time of day had irreversibly changed me. Hitting 40, I just felt like time was running out to get to where I felt I was at 30.

"I did find comfort now in church and family. Elizabeth was doing plays and sports and she never ceased to amaze me when she sang and performed at talent shows and painted. Sydney was into anything outdoors and books and building blocks. My relationship with Abby was now at its best. And church and counseling helped me slow everything down and refresh.

"But the inescapable truth was that there were fewer career days ahead than there were behind. I had lost a decade. And I was tired of paying my dues. But could a small company like ABG really light my fire in the way I needed it to be lit? Could it provide something I couldn't live without?

"When our territories realigned, we got a gentleman named Bart Phillips from Phoenix on our team. He had been with CTMI for 20 years, was two levels above my current status and knew every trick in the book of how to structure deals. He knew all of the vendors. He was really outspoken on our team calls because he would poke holes into gaps we all just kept our mouths shut about. He'd push back on the processes that made no sense, or the 'flavor of the week' things leadership was driving. He had zero filter; he was like I was at ABM, except he was in his mid-50's and just didn't care anymore. We hit it off over sushi at the conference and talked and kept in touch on instant messenger regularly.

"He saw all of the writing on the wall - the continued emphasis on call center reps and decreased attention on the real drivers of the business in the field. There was too much politics. Bart would have been a stellar manager, knowing all the ins and outs of the gig and always willing to point out changes that would help the team. I naturally bounced ideas off of him about the different role opportunities that were emerging for me. He helped me negotiate for what I wanted.

"The exercise for 'writing my dream role' was a concept I used when I wrote up what I wanted from ABG. A VP title, ownership of sales leadership, ownership of marketing, a player-coach role, direct liaison role with CTMI, and a massive base and bonus structure."

"And?"

"They didn't flinch."

"Oh, my goodness," I muttered. "Now, you've done it."

"It gets better. The most interesting play of all was on my 40th birthday when the job offer came to move to Dallas to do exactly what I wanted to do – build a brand new team for CTMI."

Chapter 9 – When it Rains, it Pours

"You can't write this stuff," I marveled. "You single-handedly created an absolute bidding war for your services and got *exactly* what you wanted. How did that come about?"

"Not the way you might think. Turns out, CTMI had some leftover budget for the back half of our fiscal year and decided to use it to hire cold-calling hunters. Full-on prospectors into our unpenetrated whitespace."

"So, they called *the* hunter!" I guessed.

"No, but after I read about it, I put myself in the mix as an interested party. I doubt anyone thought I'd move from Minneapolis. I talked it over with Abby, and she was good with me seeing it through.

"It was pretty much exactly what I did at ABM, mixed with my greatest strength at Majestech-Ware. It was the culture I came from, married with the voodoo I did better than anyone else. I told Dave Anthony I wanted it. And he very quickly got me talking to the hiring manager, Keenan Baker.

"It wasn't an easy process. Keenan drilled me about my relatively lackluster performance at CTMI since coming over from Majestech-Ware – I mean, I was under goal overall since starting despite my positive trajectory. But I had more new business driven than anyone else; more pure prospecting wins than anyone else. I had a compelling story to tell; not to mention a real platform and brand. Furthermore, I had the chops, having been a Director already at ABM, Tel-Cell and Wireless Horizons.

"That wasn't all – he practically read me verbatim the appraisal Quintana did on me when she left role and gave me zero bonus.

"I thought the interview process buried me. I took the interview remotely via video conference with three people in the Dallas office. And, irony of ironies, when I walked to lunch, Large Business Group GM Stefan Adams was walking to the same place I was, and we had the first real conversation we had ever had. He told me if I didn't get this promotion, there was a spot on his team for me."

"Unbelievable! The planets were aligning all over the place," I commented.

"I knew a change was on the horizon, but it didn't feel like I'd get what I basically now viewed as my dream job. It was much harder than I expected it to be, and I had hoped they would fall all over themselves to get me in a role that was so perfect a match.

"But I was supported overwhelmingly by a multitude of contacts I had made over the past four and a half years – I asked and received over a dozen letters of recommendation. This job was my birthright. I had to have it. And I got it.

"I was actually in Mankato on November 1, my 40th birthday, getting ready to have lunch with my parents. Abby and the kids were headed down shortly thereafter. Keenan called me and after brief small talk, he said, 'I'd love for you to come work for me and build this team. You were always my top choice.'

"Predictably, he had drilled me on that appraisal to see if I could take it and how I'd respond. Of course, you never know that in the moment – you just feel like you're being drilled because they are trying to eliminate you from the process. He had heard nothing but glowing things about me and knew that if this project was going to be successful, I was the choice.

"I was shocked to finally be moving to Dallas, but also very, very happy. I had always wanted to move to Dallas but was never able because I was a single Dad. Now, it just made sense. And Dallas had a lot more CTMI opportunities than Minneapolis did, meaning I was set up for life with this company. Director was the largest position in Minneapolis; there were VP's based in Dallas and one Senior VP. This was my dream come true.

"We found a couple of houses to look at. Jeff Mason offered to let us stay at his house while we looked at them. We found a school district in Coppell that was on par with Elizabeth's and with house prices that were only 1.5 times what we had. Heck, Elizabeth was even on board with the move. It probably didn't hurt that she had already moved schools three times while Abby and I were not together because of our various moves, and the final move when we got our house together. It was like it was meant to be. A happy ending to this sordid story.

"We told our parents. Their reactions were mixed; happy to see us advancing but sad to see us leave. Same with friends. It was surreal to realize we were leaving our house, leaving our church and Dr. Fleming and everything we had ever known. Sitting outside and basking in our backyard that fall certainly had a bittersweet feeling.

"And then the financial offer came in. Looking at a little bit more expensive house but relative parity otherwise, but a promotion to make me whole and a

Director title I expected $20K-to-$30K more per year. They offered $4,800 more plus some moving expenses. It whacked me like a club.

"Try as I might to negotiate, I couldn't even get a $10K raise for a higher cost of living. Compared to ABG, who was offering me $70K a year more than this promotion offer in base alone, plus uncapped commission and I knew how much my buddy Nick was making there, I couldn't justify moving my family that far away.

"I was super respectful to Keenan, but just broke it down for him. The accounts they had highlighted as targets – just for my existing territory alone – weren't real targets. One was with a competitor and not going anywhere. Others were only on their target list because they didn't even have enough users to be flagged as penetrated accounts. And to make comparable money to what I was making, I would in essence have to convert 25% of these suspect leads. I had to turn down the offer.

"And I actually felt some relief, at not having to leave Minnesota. It's my home. It's our home. My parents are here, Abby's parents are here. Maybe someday it will make sense. But I couldn't even justify it for my dream role.

"And after all that, my mind was made up. I told ABG in December I'd come on board March 1, 2019 when my five years at CTMI hit and all of my stock vested."

"No way!" I exclaimed, knowing full well some of the details of his career the past couple of years but certainly not these latest couple of bombshells.

"Yes. They were going to give me carte blanche to do whatever I wanted, far more money than I made at CTMI and I'd escape the politics and administrative minutiae from a company that had never made me feel welcome.

"With every passing day, I felt relief. Working with Avery - my primary sales rep – just got worse and worse. She tried to box me out of relationships I had built and nurtured for five years. The customers and vendors would just reach out to me and let me know. She talked badly about me to Jake Zuniga, who just turned right around and told me, and she'd talk bad to me about everyone else. And she was completely incompetent. She had no idea what any of our customers were doing, what their roles were, what vendors were involved. She would even try to recommend different vendors to customers while their vendor was on the phone. A complete disaster. I couldn't get away from her soon enough.

"Stefan Adams took a promotion overseas and that Large Business Group role went from being 'in the bag' for me to slowed and stalled, then non-existent.

"Then, Mick Logan took another role at a larger company and Merit Productivity tried to make a play for me to fill *his* role. The company was larger than ABG, but the money and opportunity to lead were inferior. One by one, the other contenders for me were eliminated.

"There were even overtures from our two largest competitors. But why on earth would I go do the same job I was doing now, for another company, for maybe a little more money, when my stock and brand was so good here? It had taken me five years to get to this point. I wanted to parlay my hot streak into *something better*. Had they offered me a senior role, it would have been a different story. Going elsewhere to do the same job wasn't better. The opportunity to play a major role at ABG was the right fit. I was excited.

"A lot of stress was off of me heading into 2019. I just needed to coast until March. I had it all planned out - I'd tell David officially at the beginning of February, work two weeks and take off the last two weeks of February so I could start with Accord Business Group on March 1, 2019.

"The new year brought some similar themes. Our VP, Todd Branson, asked me to present on social selling for 10 minutes to 150 people on the all-hands call. I was booked for a handful of interviews on sales podcasts to start the new year. Reps in the Large Business Group kept asking me when I was coming on board as they had heard I was. I had no expectations there.

"I actually thought once my departure from CTMI was announced that perhaps it would generate some reluctance on their part to let me go considering everything I had contributed, but it was too little, too late.

"A customer that hadn't given me the time of day for four years - a metal production company – took a meeting with one of our vendors. I liked the rep. His name was Kevin Bracken, and he had a knack for reaching out with unique outreach, like video or intel he gleaned from their LinkedIn profiles, to get their attention. He was 25 and drove a sweet black Mustang convertible. He was 'the new kind of seller.' Anyhow, he invited their CIO to TopGolf since her profile said how much she enjoyed the sport. She had never responded to my overtures in 4 years but she took this meeting. I was impressed. And I went.

"Sometimes, as a salesperson, our inclination is to look for every opportunity we can to turn the discussion toward something that will lead to a sale. Asking thinly guised questions about the business trying to uncover a gap or need. Asking about their projects and priorities. Trying to talk about our offers. But we did nothing of the sort. We bought them appetizers and drinks and hit golf balls. We learned about how long they had been there and about their families. Eventually, *they* actually brought up the fact they had ignored me for so long because CTMI audited them five years prior and we had never done anything to add value for them.

"Then they started talking about a failed data project they had done a couple of years ago and asked if maybe we wanted to come in to talk about what they had been trying to accomplish along with their roadmap. I was blown away. Patience, being opportunistic, teamwork – relying on a good vendor – and being *human* developed a potential deal, and the only thing I did in response to their olive branch was indicate that there was a lot CTMI could do to support Kevin and his company's potential work with theirs. I was nothing but an empowering agent. And that was good enough.

"Then, there was a hospital that Large Business Group had dropped down into our patch. They hadn't responded to anything I sent the first six months I covered them. The rep at the vendor who did have a relationship with them – Heath Nichols – said he was working on a deal there and it had a shot of closing sometime in 2019. Didn't really much matter since I wouldn't be there, but I kept tabs on it. It was actually January when they did finally reply to me; I used the fact that David Anthony was in town to get the meeting!

"Everything is selling, and this was no different; a lot of people try to tee up easy meetings with clients who will gush over them when the boss comes to town. I would send notes to the accounts that *wouldn't* talk to me and tell them the Director of our division was going to be in town and I'd love to get them the exposure and support. And it worked. *So* well.

"I also invited them all out to *our* office instead of going to theirs, so I could cut down on our travel time and really optimize the day. People like to get out of their office when they can, and I could give them a tour, show them hospitality - the whole nine.

"One day I lined up 11 meetings for Dave Anthony and me, and the next day a half dozen more. And it got a response from the hospital, the metal production company where we had a burgeoning relationship and a handful of others I had little to no relationship with.

"FitSmart opted to go another route for their new parent company's solution, which was unfortunate. However, I saw steady climbs at a FinTech startup that ghosted me my first 3 years in role. One of my financial organizations made an acquisition that doubled our contract. I had one quarter left in this job, and it looked like it was going to be a great one.

"Then, given his desire to keep me on the team, David Anthony got approval to promote me in March to Sr. Territory Manager. A midyear promotion was rare, but I was trending now to hit 110% for the year, my street cred was good and reputation and brand strong and they decided I was worthy."

I-62 turned into CR-32 as we headed into Lynnhurst. It was nearing 3 PM. Vincent drove by several nice neighborhoods. The tree coverage was spectacular, and they showed precursor to signs of bloom. Not quite there yet, as Minneapolis typically sees its spring after the rest of the states. It was thankfully nice enough – *just* nice enough – for the top on the convertible to be down.

"So, I figured the least I could do before I take you to the airport is give you a home-cooked meal," Vincent said. "I'll show you the place. The place I wouldn't leave for a lackluster promotion," he chuckled.

"You are too kind, good sir," I replied.

Vincent's house was respectable, a nice one-story Spanish-style near a park and trail in the middle of Lynnhurst, MN. Another car was in the garage, presumably Abby's. Vincent pulled into the open spot, put the top back up on the convertible and we exited.

The garage was the first and immediate sign of other life; interesting since the last time I delved into this man's life he lived in a one-bedroom apartment and was a single Dad. There were bicycles large and small. Rollerblades, a full tool bench and some decorations, folding chairs and bins for the dog and cat food.

He led me around the house, where we saw the basketball goal on the back porch, the hot tub, the spacious lawn framed perfectly by towering trees. He spoke with pride about the place, his affinity for mowing the lawn and playing outside (specifically playing basketball with Elizabeth and blowing bubbles with Sydney) and what a grilling master his wife was.

144

One of the neighbors – Jay Cavill – also popped out from next door to say hello and shoot a couple of baskets with us before we headed inside.

I had met everyone but Sydney previously, so we exchanged greetings. Abby was currently a stay-at-home Mom taking care of 3-year old Sydney. Elizabeth was in middle school, in sixth grade. Vincent and his family lived modestly for the success he had enjoyed.

After a bit of conversation, Abby assuring me that I'd very much enjoy the dinner of salmon, potatoes and vegetables, and Elizabeth going to finish her homework while Sydney watched *Mickey Mouse Clubhouse*, Vincent led me down the stairs into the basement.

It was dark in the basement, but he sped his pace to the other end of the room. Shortly thereafter, the room lit up. Most prominently I could see the lights over a bar and a blue and pink neon light announcing, "Cocktails & Dreams."

"I love it!" I proclaimed. "The neon from *Cocktail*. You wrote an article about that movie once."

"Yes, I did – one of the greatest sales movies ever made, that most people don't view as a sales movie."

"I remember," came my reply.

He motioned to the barstools and took a place behind the bar.

"What can I get you?" he inquired. "A vodka specialty, perhaps?"

"I see you have Johnnie Walker Blue," I remarked.

"Yes, my birthday present from me to me," he replied, fishing the bottle from its place behind the bar and nabbing two glasses from their resting place. The glasses bore the insignia "VTS"

"Your initials?" I asked.

"These were my late paternal grandfather's, whom I never met. I got these, this ashtray, his cufflinks and his bowling ball," Vincent recounted. "Even bowled three strikes in a row the first three frames I threw it."

"Nice," I offered, taking in the full view of his bar. It was adorned with pictures, awards, memorabilia. It was clear his tastes for sports, cars, and film. He also had drawings from his kids. There were a few items I couldn't quite pin down the meaning behind.

Vincent poured us a generous amount apiece of the dark liquid; more in my glass than his. "I'm driving," he explained.

"So, walk me through the scene," I requested, gesturing toward his bar and its many adornments.

He walked toward the other end of the bar. En route, he stopped and held his glass out in my direction.

"To health and friendship," he said, with a twinkle in his eye.

"Life and love," I replied. We clinked glasses and took a sip.

Vincent pointed out a few things on the end. There were obvious ones, like a Michael Jordan jersey (ironically from when he was on the Wizards – Vincent explained this was because everyone has the vintage Bulls one but this one signified reinvention and a third run, sometimes as a role player), autographed pictures of all of the James Bond actors, a sign from the show *Cheers* (Vincent professed his affinity for bartender Sam Malone) and some trophies – from things like bowling, basketball and baseball, to a medal from a Majestech-Ware 5K, an award from ABM for the Top Gun Award and an MVP plaque from Majestech-Ware. There were tracings from his kids and pictures of them as well.

"Here's a picture from Rainier," he said. It showed him with Dan Winters, Jamie Winters and Robert Earley, in a section of overlook with the backdrop of the majestic peak.

Then he pointed out a Minnesota Twins clock. "This is from 'The Cheetah,' which was basically a gentleman's cigar and whiskey club in a treehouse."

"Do tell."

"In high school, a friend of mine – Mark Gartner – had this treehouse on his parents' property near Mankato. It was big enough to fit about 10 of us on a good night. Those were some of the best days of our lives – we'd climb up there, listen to Sinatra, enjoy a cigar and a few drinks and talk about everything – girls, school, the future. We would always etch our names in the boards for each Cheetah night. And, eventually, he retired it when his parents moved and sold the property. It was torn down. I got the clock."

I didn't say anything. Vincent was in full reminiscing mode. His eyes went next to a picture; I could clearly see him, clinking glasses with some others.

"Here are some of those folks right here," Vincent smiled, picking up the picture and rubbing any hints of dust from it. "The college days. That's Eddie, that's Jack, that's Julie, Gus and Justin. We had many a night together back in those days. We thought we'd run the world someday."

There was a jersey from Minnesota State University, Mankato. "That was a practice jersey from the team. I never played college ball. Could have walked on, but I knew I'd never go pro. I miss playing. One of my few regrets in life is not playing more basketball, not trying harder at some of the things I'll never have a chance to do again."

Lots more stuff from the Minnesota Vikings and Twins and even the North Stars. There was a cup from a World Series game he had attended, a ticket from a Super Bowl he had attended. A copy of his first book. Newspaper clippings featuring profiles of him when the book had come out. A script from the movie *Cocktail* along with a Care Bear and dinosaur Vincent revealed Abby had gotten him (they were all featured in their bar in the movie). And several model cars – Aston Martin, DeLorean from *Back to the Future* and the Formula One car for Aston Martin Red Bull.

To the side, there were small booklets that were from funerals. I could see the pictures of the deceased.

"This was my Grandpa, on my Mom's side. He died when I was 22 and had just started at ABM. This was Abby's Grandpa. This was John Propst, who dated my Grandma for several years after my Grandpa died.

"And this was my aunt, Victoria Scott Quincy. My Dad's sister. She died January 1, 2019."

"I'm sorry to hear that," I offered.

"Thanks," he replied. "I had not seen her a lot over the few decades since my youth, but fortunately did a couple of times in her last two years. She and most of her kids and their kids lived in and near Milwaukee. For whatever reason, I didn't really travel there often. But with her passing, I saw a lot of my cousins for the first time in a long time and I was very thankful for that.

"Family is everything. Love is everything. Friends. Passion for something. The older I get, the more I realize how important it is to have these things worth fighting for. I questioned my passion a lot these last couple of years. 2019 was a challenging year – like no other. This year has been even more so, albeit in different ways. But I'm thankful for the time, as I've gotten a lot more perspective and clarity.

"At the beginning of 2019, we started reading the Bible in its entirety. I had read it when I was a kid – I read everything I could get my hands on. I was addicted to the Oz books by L. Frank Baum and continuation writers. As I got older, it was Bond and Holmes. But Abby and I read the entire Bible in 2019 – day by day by day.

"I started having coffees with our vicar and a church elder. It was wonderful to have two men near my age with families of their own with whom to share our successes and struggles.

"Starting 2019, I had a little 'post party depression' like Ted Danson calls it in *Three Men and a Baby*," Vincent said wryly. "The holidays are awesome, and then there's just this end of it all. The tree comes down, decorations come down. Life and school and work resumes. And I have the annual task of having to top what I did the year prior.

"The start of 2019, I went in fully knowing that I was leaving for Accord in just two short months. There was some benefit to that.

"I have what I call 'merger mentality'," Vincent continued, taking another sip of his drink. I followed suit, realizing I was so enthralled with the story that I had been slacking. "Even when I know I am moving on to something else or another role, I operate as if it will not happen – like a merger is supposed to transpire. Both organizations have to operate as if the merger will not happen so as to not negatively impact either company's trajectory. I also had a bonus coming and stock vesting, so I was perfectly timing my March 1 departure.

"As I mentioned, I was also mixing it up with a lot of podcast appearances around that time. Those were always fun. I found that work would occasionally have me weary, but I came alive in those discussions – talking about sales and leadership and my passion for the sport.

"I started sleep-walking through my day job. I was back to being like Neo in *The Matrix*; everything was starting to come so easily. I was wheeling and dealing, was earning funding from the council with brilliantly woven stories and was being called in to clean up Avery's messes. I had known a lot of these vendors and customers for five years and they had come to trust me. Heck, I even introduced one to our competitor Apricot Innovations on a hardware deal because I had a lot of contacts over there. So, when Avery tried to put the screws on these customers by not discounting their deals and not having a clue what their initiatives were, they called me.

"It was a struggle to stay detached, but fortunately my role was to create and craft a lot of these deals. She would try to keep me at arm's length, to her detriment, but fortunately I had Dave Anthony's blessing to basically do whatever I wanted. So, when she screwed up a deal with a nonsensical spiel that confused a CIO, I called them after the call and constructed a deal myself. I got it blessed by Dave and got us all paid – Avery included. Had she been left in charge, we would have missed quota on the account and lost a lot of face on the flubbed deal.

"Another customer, one of the Minnesota railways, had a deal renewal coming up. Avery would always try to force me out of renewals saying it was her primary purview and I should only focus on net new. But you could land some of the most strategic upsells including new KPI's during renewal, and I had all of the relationships and deal-making and negotiating skills, so it was to everyone's benefit to have me involved – if not leading – those efforts.

"That said, she would schedule calls with these customers and vendors without even inviting me. And she tried to strong-arm the customers, attempting to get them to sign up for these box check assessments without explaining them, trying to add solutions and features to their deal without explaining them, and when they'd balk she'd claim the customers weren't strategic and she failed in her internal bid to get them any kind of discount. That, ultimately, infuriated the customers. She didn't understand the customer need, she didn't listen, she did not pay attention to informed vendor recommendations, and she couldn't sell the story internally. She wasn't a good partner.

"Avery would go round and round with customers and partners. It was really quite painful to witness. On the one hand, I could absolutely go behind her back and take over the deal that was rightfully just as much mine anyway. But by biding my time, the customers came to me and when they did, they needed me. There was already the defined need of renewing services and potential gaps in their business, but their other need was *me*.

"Full transparency and taking them on the journey with me, with us, was really all it took. The railway bought everything I wanted them to. I had an uncanny ability of taking a look at where they wanted to be, where they thought they needed to be, and assessing the financials and their budget. Then I'd surmise what I thought I could feasibly add to the deal, based on what I thought they'd actually use, what would benefit them and what would get CTMI paid – which, in turn, they would allow me to discount generously. Customers are willing to pay a little more than anticipated for true value, but you have to construct it in a respectful, collaborative way.

"It had become too easy. I could do this in my sleep – get their buy-in to the numbers and what services they thought should be attached, and then weave in what I wanted, gain them a healthy discount and funding dollars and ink a deal where everybody wins. It turned into one of the few things about my job I enjoyed.

"Working with Avery was a pain and just got increasingly worse. She'd get her boss, Nancy, involved, and basically tell her I was overstepping my bounds. This resulted in Nancy scheduling calls with both of us to get to the bottom of it and she would come in under that impression before I'd talk her down and explain the holistic way I managed things.

"Then, Nancy's boss, Arthur, was regarded like he was the big bad wolf; they were all afraid to go to him for discounting or for any type of deal review. I wasn't. If he was the one who had to approve it and I knew it was the right deal for all parties, I had no qualms about taking it straight to him even though Avery was supposed to.

"And there came a time when Arthur wondered why I was always the one coming to him for these deals rather than Avery. It was a valid question. And when Avery was on these deal reviews, and I'd do all the talking, and she had absolutely no idea what she was talking about or really anything at all about the customer, it was glaringly obvious she was terrible at her job. This further drove a wedge between her and me. And it led her to do more and more to try to undermine me or claim I overstepped my bounds. But fortunately, I didn't need her or anything from her. Quite the opposite of her situation – she was completely dependent on me. Her results were stellar because of what I had achieved. And my stock was high enough that no matter what knocks she tried to make on my way of doing things, they didn't matter. Nobody cared or listened.

"There were two separate and distinct entities vying for control within CTMI and it was destined for a meltdown. The traditional field organization – legacy Majestech-Ware, which I was a part of - reporting up to Dave Anthony, then his

150

relatively new boss John Lewis, and his boss – VP Todd Branson – was the original business. Janet Leary had literally just left for a healthcare vendor startup, and John had come on at the end of 2018.

"Legacy CTMI had always had this inside sales division, and now the same accounts carried overhead from two business units. CTMI inside sales preached to their people that they *owned* these accounts. I hate that territorial nonsense – nobody owns accounts, especially when a dozen people get paid on them. In fact, every single time I talk to anyone internal or even a vendor, I ask how I can either empower or support them to win in *our mutual account.*"

"I love that," I remarked. "It really all boils down to wording and psychology, doesn't it?"

"Exactly. People just need to feel like they belong and you're there to help them. It changes the whole dynamic of a relationship. I tried with Avery, but she chose instead to be divisive and standoffish and make me an enemy. She talked badly about everyone behind their backs and because she was so disliked, they all knew. And it was a culture thing; most of these inside sales folks were so short-sighted on one individual discussion or deal going their way. They failed to look at the big picture. If you want a customer to give you all of their data, you have to give them something along the way – a show of good faith on the first deal or the second. They'll bet big on you if you invest in them.

"On the other hand, Avery's incompetence actually elevated my brand even further in CTMI. I'd be asked to be part of sessions that technically fell outside of my scope. For example, we had a design and construction firm in St. Paul to whom my team had sold everything in years past. Even though there was no more net new to be had, I had all of the relationships with the C-Suite. So, when we were attempting to gain more standing and partnership with them, I was asked by the growth team to lead the initiative. I obliged. And I sold them a lot more.

"I became known as the Deal Whisperer. I was crafting these magical deals left and right, making strategic attachments to renewal motions, conjuring up net new logos with clients that had ignored me in years past. And my side hustle was thriving – a dozen podcast interviews in the first quarter of the year. What had been a pretty solid last 18 months was now beginning to inexplicably surge.

"The inevitable time came... Darren Miller and Shawn Wiseman told me they would be reaching out in January 2019 to initiate the formal process of me joining

Accord Business Group. It bled into February, and by then my forecast for the fiscal year was starting to look really strong. The data project with the mining company that started at TopGolf was gaining a little traction, albeit with a lot of milestones and conversations to hit but it was in my sights. The hospital project Heath Nichols was working on had turned out to be nowhere near done, but based on multiple conversations I had now had with their CIO it sounded like there was at least interest in making a deal happen. The California airline deal from a year ago was even possibly resuscitated. I found myself actually hoping I *wouldn't* hear anything from Accord."

"Oh boy," I muttered. "Isn't that how it always happens?"

"Nothing ever goes the way you think it will," Vincent agreed.

Chapter 10 – The Home Stretch

"Do you want to play UNO?" he asked, quite out of the blue, revealing a deck of the cards from behind the bar.

"Sure," I laughed. I hadn't played UNO in some time, but love the game.

Vincent removed the somewhat worn cards from their box and began to shuffle them.

"Not quite Bond's baccarat Chemin-de-fer, but this game always reminds me of my Dad. We play every time I see him. And now I play it with Abby and Elizabeth sometimes, too."

His demeanor was just different when he talked about family and friends and good memories. When the topic was work, he was very business-like – almost clinical. I could tell he had perfected this ability to turn off his emotions when the subject of work was afoot.

Vincent dealt and we began to play. I could tell that despite the fact his story continued, and we were playing a zero stakes card game he was studying the cards played and was deliberate in his game play. A competitor always.

"So, 2019 started off pretty fast and furious. I found that the first half of the fiscal year was really good for prospecting, having conversations, planting pipeline. The back half, I was laser-focused on 'the deals.' I had 43 deals I had to close the back half of the year.

"We did our forecast session in Dallas to kick off February, and my forecast was very strong. It changed everything about the way I thought about leaving. Dave Anthony also promoted me, meaning a 'Senior' title, more money, more stock. And if I could do the unthinkable and pull off some of these deals, I'd far surpass what Accord had offered me. My 110% trend to goal looked to be a vast understatement.

"It was Monday, February 11 when I broke it to them. I just couldn't justify leaving anymore. I hate disappointing people. It didn't help that I had told them in December that I was coming on board. But I just couldn't leave. It didn't feel right. It was not the best move for my family or career anymore.

"I didn't really know the path I was on – the direction of my division or territory or really anything. But the past few years, as I've had other organizations vie – sometimes aggressively – for me, I compare the opportunity to the exact current situation and the trajectory. Based on my forecast and the probability of a strong year, I couldn't make a move. So, I stayed – to Dave Anthony's delight.

"Each time I faced one of these decisions was quite introspective and insightful for me – it enlightened me to my own true priorities. I knew I wanted to stay in Minneapolis. If I was a younger, single guy, I would have left for Dallas already. But staying put was now a must. Furthermore, I wanted to get back into mid-management, but no one was offering me that outside of the vendor community. I preferred the prestige of a brand name, especially considering I was trying to build my own brand. Maybe a few years down the road I'd come across the right vendor opportunity, but right now I was gaining experience and trying to gain notoriety in a big business.

"And now I had a unique opportunity – to stay the course and have a banner year. A year that would eradicate the memory of what Quintana said about me. If I left, I would always wonder if what she said had some truth to it, and maybe others would, too. I couldn't leave in the midst of this comeback.

"Either way, I was going to leave it all on the field.

"Dave Anthony was traveling in March and came through the Twin Cities again. I took my same approach: utilizing the presence of the Sr. Director of our division to offer exposure to him as an incentive for customers who didn't usually take meetings with me to do so. This time, it worked again to the tune of another 10 meetings across a day and a half. They were *all* a hit.

"There was a fabrication business who had tussled with us over invoices and inconsistency in the relationship over the years – and we partnered on an IoT project. One of our credit card processing customers had made an acquisition, and we came out of these talks with a deal that would *double* their business with us. A vendor of ours who did limited business with us and more with our competitors emerged as interested in partnering on a project together and a net new agreement. Another health provider agreed to pursue a POC on a data project for one of their government contracts. We found a surveillance project with a security company I had never been able to talk to. Even a metal trading company who had traditionally not been fans of ours agreed to a pilot. The list goes on. And none of this stuff had already been in forecast or pipeline.

"What was most encouraging to me was my confidence level in leading these sessions. I barely even relied on Dave to speak this time around, which was a stark contrast to the less confident version of me when we started working together. Sure – me using his presence was what helped me create the meeting. But I used it as a means to an end – to get in front of these folks, evangelize our brand and the resources we could leverage on their behalf, and to really help ensure they understood our story and how we wanted to help. I could talk the talk.

"No matter the conversation, I could turn off my doubt and my brain. I could speak quickly and articulate what I want to articulate, and thanks to just being in the room over the years to soak in the pearls of wisdom, I could regurgitate enough stories and vision to get interest and sound passable enough to craft a lively dialogue. I could also type fast enough and take notes comprehensively enough to map out an extensive follow-up plan.

"That's what I've realized sales is. Using every tool at your disposal to find prospects and get meetings. Staying top of mind. And asking the right questions and telling the right stories to keep the discussion alive, hitting milestones and leading toward a deal. I thought I was a good seller in my 20's, but I didn't even scratch the surface until 40.

"There are good days and there are insane days. But you just have to get through the day, one milestone and one meeting at a time. Map it out, but slow it down – call by call, task by task.

"Avery continued to make things difficult, but often opened up opportunities for me to be the hero. Furthermore, nothing would *ever* go off without a hitch.

"The credit card company where we found a way to double our revenue had political infighting because the acquired company was proving more valuable than the parent company and egos got involved. They tried to pull me into the fray, and it compromised my relationship with the parent company's CEO. They wanted me to pick sides so our dealings would favor one company over the other, but I had to remain diplomatic all the way. And I did – I pulled both CEO's together for a meeting and laid out how this was going to work and why we had to work together in the best interests of their overall organization. How they decided to split up our resources was their call, but I was happy to make some recommendations.

"The metal trading organization wanted to use a specific vendor, but that vendor was not qualified to do the work – so we brought in someone else and that ticked off both parties! Then we couldn't even give them funding, because they were under an audit. Turns out I could have called off the audit had the customer even been talking to us previously, but without open lines of communication I had no reason to. This further angered the customer. Disaster.

"The big hospital project got more and more complicated; we leveraged multiple vendors to help plan our recommended go-forward strategy, met with dozens of senior leaders and employees, mapped out an extensive roadmap, and started mocking up pricing – that they balked at. They wanted to avoid going to their board at all costs, which was going to take serious finagling and creativity on my part. And they couldn't even guarantee my efforts would equate to a deal.

"The hairiest situation was the renewal with Bill Process Management. My relationship with Charles Royal and Shane Madden had grown quite strong. I got them connected to a vendor who was streamlining all of their data applications on our platform and creating a data lake. This had the potential to be a $5 million deal over the next few years. Heavy work was underway. But their core applications through us – which were significant but one-fifth the opportunity – were up for renewal. And Avery was trying to strong-arm them with no discount whatsoever at renewal because they weren't adding anything at that moment.

"I had upsold them a year ago into a cloud-enabled version of our product and extended them a healthy discount because they were not able to move right away on the upgrades. They were concerned with ensuring they could get a good discount at renewal, and I informed them that while I couldn't make any promises, we'd absolutely take a holistic approach on their strategic direction with us in negotiating that deal. They were on board with that – and we all assumed I'd be the one negotiating the deal. Yet when the inside sales team encroached on our business and told their people they owned the accounts, they tried to take full ownership of negotiating renewals. Fine.

"However, as I've already shared, they were rubbing customers the wrong way. BPM was no different. But Charles was trying to get me to get involved; I'd prod Avery to take better care of them, but she ignored my suggestions. The renewal was due in May, and conversations had started in January, but they were at a standstill with the deadline near.

"Bottom line, they had reasonably budgeted for a certain level of increase in costs and Avery was trying to give them no discount whatsoever on the new deal because they were not currently adding to their solution set. We were building a data platform together, but that deal would not be realized until next fiscal year. So, she was holding their feet to the fire to make more money – and likely because she did not have the wherewithal to take a proper incentive request to her superiors. The whole situation stunk.

"Another point of contention was I actually was trying to negotiate a couple of extra bells and whistles that would help them get discounting plus get CTMI paid. It was mutually beneficial stuff – they were using some light versions of those features already, but Avery was trying to block me saying the customer didn't need it. She didn't get it. At all. And whatever semblance of functionality Avery and I had in our working relationship went kaput with the BPM deal.

"Eventually, her boss and her boss's boss had to get involved. And they even told BPM CEO Charles Royal to write them an e-mail implicitly saying I had given them an illegal discount promise a year prior that we'd extend at this renewal. He called me and told me all about it, as did the vendor. Then the stuff really hit the fan."

"Unbelievable!" I marveled, enjoying another sip of my drink. He did the same. "What in the world were they thinking?"

"I'll never know," he remarked. "And I was extremely upset by it. After everything I had done to rebuild my brand here, Arthur, Nancy and Avery were attempting to get one of my better customer relationships to turn on me. I can only assume that they wanted to use it as an internal bargaining chip to not take it on the chin when they extended a discount and make my department eat it. Instead, they'd get me fired or written up, and my field team would have to take the commission cut.

"I took it and my concerns straight to Dave Anthony. For me to *not* publicly call out Arthur or do anything to cover myself took every bit of restraint I had. Dave said he would handle it, and I left it at that. I did, however, start and delete an e-mail to Arthur multiple times addressing what he had attempted to do to me.

"But when the dust settled, Avery's skip level Arthur had to call me, hat in hand, and ask me to go out and close this deal. He gave me carte blanche to do it however I saw fit. And I got what they couldn't do in six months closed in 45 minutes. Charles Royal even sent a note to our VP Todd Branson, our GM John Lewis, Dave Anthony, Arthur, Avery's boss Nancy and other members of CTMI account team and the vendor team praising me."

I bellowed. "Are you serious?"

"It was easy," he said, nonchalantly. "I asked them what their budget was and understood where they needed to be and why. Heck, they were also trying to budget for a future $5 million project with us! We found a happy medium, I added the additional products that got my team paid and we got a commitment on the other data project. They were reasonable people agreeable to a fair increase – they just didn't want to be manhandled. They paid a little more, we came down substantially, and everyone walked away happy. Except probably Avery, even though thanks to me she was the #1 rep in her division for the year. Oh well."

"We can't please them all," I mused. "How ungrateful."

"Yeah, I'm used to it. She was more combative and standoffish and back-stabbing than anything. She literally came to Minneapolis *one* time to visit customers because Accord of all partners have this annual summit for business leaders. She got drunk the night prior with one of the partners and showed up extremely late. She even tried to lecture me on how to sell or start negotiating deals, using these examples where we fought as a signal I must need help – and I closed large deals she couldn't in every case – as examples!

"She got mad because I introduced a partner to do a data project with a customer that happened to have a renewal coming up, accusing me of overstepping my bounds and involving myself in her responsibility. It didn't matter I had known the customer forever, this wasn't at all related to their renewal of existing products, and I knew the partner ecosystem. She just wanted to claim I was in her way so she could control the situation, even if she drove it into the toilet. Problem is, I could have just not told her what I was doing, but transparency and teamwork are in my nature.

"But, knowing this, I had to make a difficult decision. I *did* intentionally start excluding her from as much as I could get away with. I called a CIO after a meeting she botched once and orchestrated a substantial deal. I sure as heck proceeded with the pending hospital deal and pending other net new deals without even telling her what was going on. When she did ask – which, sadly was rare – I was vague. It was all 'need to know' and she didn't need to know."

We laughed a bit about that.

"I'm telling you, I've learned more in my career and in selling from my losses than anything else. How to play the political game, how to pick my battles. Plus, I learned every single little step I needed to take from a milestone perspective in some of these gruesome deals where we had 11th hour surprises!

"My year was going to be good – there was no doubt about it. We had closed a basic deal with a resort in Florida earlier in the year and due to strong results, they placed a sizable order in April. There were a handful of renewals I was able to substantially grow by getting involved and negotiating additional product. But the hospital deal was going to be the one that took it to a whole other level. Large Business Group had chased this deal for 3 years and if I could somehow get it done, I would be a hero.

"Knowing where other large deals had gone awry helped. Knowing who I needed to pull into the sales team with me helped. I made sure the vendor got them blank contracts in April to review with legal with plenty of time to go. We bandied around hypothetical numbers, did a workshop together that gave members of every segment of their hospital exposure to what our platform did and could do for them, understood when their board met, understood the deal threshold that didn't have to be reviewed by the board, you name it.

"Prior to me offering up a Dave Anthony lunch with the CIO and IT Director only the vendor had a real relationship with these folks – I was the first person at CTMI to really break ground here. And even though they didn't treat me like their best friend just yet, they were getting a little more forthcoming with each dialogue. The deal had legs but there was a lot more to do. But anything that had ever held me up in the final stages of any deal I had done in the past, I knew to nip in the bud here before it ever even became a problem."

"How did you get to the table where others didn't?"

"It was a couple of things," he replied. "Sure - floating the in-town presence of Sr. Director of commercial sales Dave Anthony was part of it. But the other part was knowing these guys had a need and ensuring to wrap up our and my unique role in that need. There's a benefit to knowing the intricate details of how to leverage incentives and licensing and funding to everyone's advantage. The customer saves, the vendor gets paid and we get a new logo. I could strategically offer up my willingness and ability to navigate those waters on their behalf. I could make sure they knew they would not get the best deal possible unless we were involved, partly by enticing them with examples of value adds I could make available to them. If they knew they had to work with me to do what was best for their organization, I had a seat at the table."

"Makes perfect sense," I responded. "How did you avoid any potential roadblocks?"

"Part of the trick to that was arriving at a final configuration of a deal. For the mining company deal, I never actually thought it was going to happen until they had some personnel changes and the new folks were receptive. The TopGolf session happened, they enjoyed the vendor relationship they were having, and I did everything I could to empower that.

"If they liked the vendor, cool – I could funnel my support and funding through them and will them to win. We got paperwork submitted and prepared in May...and the customer said their legal process would take about a month... and so we wait. The Area Manager at that vendor actually dissed me behind my back to others at CTMI and to her own leadership, saying I was the reason she couldn't bring that deal home in May – she expected me to somehow strong-arm them on the timeline and get it done anyway, but that wasn't my style and last I checked you don't 'strong-arm' legal. She was wrong.

"But arriving at a final deal configuration for the hospital was difficult because they wanted to keep adding things but keep the total investment under $6 million.

"I eventually arrived at a place where I believed I could get every deal done except that hospital. It would be a virtual repeat of last year. Respectable. Good. But not supreme.

"The nice thing is other areas of my life were good. I would still get recognized from time to time in public for my books or podcasts I had appeared on. I was asked to present on a panel in downtown Minneapolis with some other luminaries of sales who were traveling in for the session and I actually spoke more and was asked more questions than any of the others. There's a fun element in being a very, very minor celebrity – where it doesn't interrupt your life but there's some occasional referendum that you've done good work or impacted others in a positive way. I'm sure you know what I mean."

"No, I have no idea." We chuckled. "That's a shame, really – that you did so much, made so much progress, only to have an admirable year that wasn't a full-on blowout. I know you wanted to kill it."

"We were assigned quota across multiple buckets – namely, new logos, cloud revenue, security packages, internal data and collaboration, and artificial intelligence. The team had knocked all of them out of the park except one – the overall cloud revenue one, which had a lot of eyes on it. The hospital could put us there.

"But, with that deal looking unlikely, it was still full steam ahead. Plenty to do. It's funny, you think you have two months to get a deal done, but the reality is a month is 20 to 22 sales days. It takes several days or a week to get a response or get something processed. A month will evaporate in no time at all. There is never time to waste; to get some deals done it takes all year.

"Win, lose or draw, though, I was glad I stayed put. It was another decent year and I'd get paid OK. Dave Anthony liked me so at least I'd get a bonus this year, as opposed to the Quintana calamity. Abby and I booked a trip to Jamaica for July. I was ready for a reset. Needed to unplug and truly unwind again.

"The benefit of being in this gig for a little bit and knowing how long it took to do some of these deals was that I was *so* proactive I had some of them getting across in May. The airline deal came through – after two years of hammering that thing out. It was positioned for three years with an upfront payment but including payment arrangements, so we got the money and revenue realization upfront. I got them a boatload of post-sale funding to help the vendor build the custom solution. They would be tracking predictive maintenance on all the planes, tracking routes and takeoffs more efficiently and the return on investment was more potential flights and customer satisfaction.

"There was an energy holding company I'd been chasing for two years as well, with whom I managed to empower a vendor to get a nice net new deal. Total surprise. It took doing, because their legal team had to comb through stuff and I was worried it would take some time, but I got that one in, too.

"I was also pleasantly surprised that the mining company's legal team approved that deal early and I got it in in May also – which I very subtly rubbed in the vendor manager's face for claiming I was the reason for delay."

We laughed.

"And then *her* team failed to get the PO for two weeks, causing a delay!"

"You can't make this stuff up!" I exclaimed.

"The big hotel deal invoiced and processed first week of June.

161

"And suddenly the hospital deal became the last one standing. And it just kept getting whittled down, little by little.

"I pushed to get it done early if it was going to happen. They kept trying to finagle for more product for less money. I bent over backwards to deliver it under $6 million so it wouldn't go to their board and delivered exactly what they asked for, only to have them try to get me to add more product.

"I had given them a cutoff of June 21 if they wanted the deal done. And they pushed beyond. That last week would be cutting it close, because the last business day of the year was June 28 – a Friday.

"Everything else completed for the year, I was feverishly working on this deal – working off spreadsheets, slicing and dicing discounts across different SKU's. The hospital's biggest source of contention was that they wouldn't fully be able to embrace our solution in the first year because of other initiatives. I got my VP Todd Branson to approve an aggressive year one discount that would taper off over three years. It all looked good.

"Then the vendor misquoted them at lower SKU rates, leaving us scrambling because the hospital wanted us to honor that price and I couldn't. So, I had to go back to the spreadsheet board...getting creative. I found a way to qualify them for a better pricing bracket by adding more of a specific SKU and then I offered a deeper discount. The percentages were a bit more absurd than I originally wanted, but I made the case to the VP and I got it approved. I always got everything approved. If you effectively advocate for your customers and your employees, and you can sell leadership on why it's got to happen – it will.

"But instead of just taking it back to them, I had asked 'if I can get this approved, will you sign?' I had no more opportunity for them to modify the deal. They said they'd have to get CEO approval but that yes – it was what they needed to get the deal done. So, I went back to them with the approved structure and assumed it would be done by Friday, June 28. Things were looking up. I suddenly had a real shot of getting this done. There was a slim opening, but an opening nonetheless.

"It was Wednesday of that week when I had three crippling setbacks and another customer who reached out to my CEO."

"Oh boy," I muttered.

Chapter 11 – Sunset

"11th hour setbacks?" I asked.

"To the nth degree," Vincent replied, finishing the last of his drink. As he was driving me to the airport shortly, he did not have another but offered me one. I obliged.

"And I just had to get the deal across. *I had to*. I was getting hourly status update request calls from Dave Anthony. The business unit was not going to hit their number unless I got this deal – even though I was already the top performer at close to 120%.

"A critical CFO meeting was supposed to take place that Wednesday, but the CIO was inexplicably off work. His top guy, the IT Director, sent us back a note saying they wanted an amendment to our contract spelling out certain language about where their data would physically reside in certain circumstances even though we had already published that information on our website. There was no flexibility to the contract, and even if there was you can't do it beyond a deadline when it takes our legal team another week to even review the proposed revisions.

"I had to stress to him that the deal was the deal at this point and I couldn't get the contract terms changed lest we were completely back at square one with a brand new deal in a new fiscal year with completely different terms and no chance at the same pricing. What I had managed to get them at $6 million would have been $8 million over the same term under any other set of circumstances.

"Then they asked about a not-to-exceed clause. Another wrinkle, another conversation that had to be held. Of course, I could handle that in stride because a clause like that would be considered a high concession and would eradicate the meaty discount I had gotten them. Next.

"These are also often the moments when the team scatters. The people you've brought into the boat are either nowhere to be found or they just muddy the waters. The contract specialist I had consulted sent a pretty blunt response to the customer, which didn't make them happy. The job of a seller isn't just to get the meeting and grow the relationship, it's often to put the positive spin on the company line and come up with the outside the box solution to make everyone happy.

"Then the contract team made a mistake, not discounting a specific SKU as we had agreed and the final package that went out for signature had the wrong price on it. So, I had to reach out to them myself to get it fixed.

"Believe me, it would have been nice if Avery was competent enough or trustworthy enough to be along for the ride up to this point, because I really could have used a good rep. But I had cut her out, so it was just me. One of the other guys who got paid on this deal – Joe Silver – also worked in the call center and was the worst when it came to responsiveness and follow-up. He could most likely be found at the ping pong table. It was up to me.

"And, at 5:02 PM, after fighting to get the final package out for signature, defending why we couldn't modify the terms but trying to put them at ease on our publicly published terms and conditions, wondering if the critical CIO-CFO meeting had taken place to ensure smooth sailing to the CEO and having to go back and forth with the contracts team to actually make sure the right contract was going to them, the President of the FinTech startup I had signed after three years of their standoffish behavior sent an e-mail to our CEO because Avery had failed in properly escalating their support issues and I was too preoccupied with bringing home all 42 of the other second half deals to get involved in yet another thing that wasn't my job."

He paused for a moment. I could tell he was contemplating another drink. He opted for a Perrier instead.

"Unbelievable," I remarked, shaking my head. "How do you do it and retain composure?"

"There's a lot of cursing to myself sometimes, fortunately while I'm alone in an office," Vincent smiled. He shook his head. "It's remarkable, because I wasn't able to handle that level of frustration to *that* degree in my ABM days when I *thought* I was at my best and unflappable.

"No, I would have just tried to ram the deal home and it wouldn't have worked. I never dealt with deals of this caliber. We were selling little advertising programs for $39 a month up to occasionally thousands and rarely hundreds of thousands of dollars. But it was a one-call close numbers game and if you didn't get this deal or that deal, there was always the next one. Here, there are so many more variables. I have to stay true to my core, which is customer, company and me. My team. Knowing I have those responsibilities helps me keep a steady hand on the wheel. Steady-*ish*."

We laughed.

"That's why being a parent and now a husband made me better at everything. Being a better leader, better seller. Better man. More patient. More empathetic. I was able to think about others *far* more than myself.

"There's only so much you can control. And if you go into situations or days with little to no expectation, you're rarely disappointed. You approach each milestone or critical moment individually, throwing your focus into it only when it warrants it. Certainly, surprises can catch you completely off guard, but that's when you pivot. If you're agile, you can manage. If you're flexible, you can turn on a dime and move in the new direction.

"Parenting is like that. Your kid or kids will never do exactly what you think you want them to do no matter what foundation or guidelines you set in place. They'll do something else, but it's still beautiful. I always hoped Elizabeth would want to play sports, but she showed no interest for a long time and we didn't force her. She excelled, though, at singing, art, painting, crafts, writing. And she eventually got into sports anyway. Who in the world would be upset with that? She makes her own art, and that's beautiful. And that's the way I look about sales.

"It's never going to give me exactly what I think I want. You think I wanted to get fired from ABM? You think I wanted to lose every friend I thought I had and live 3 years in relative exile bouncing around making a fraction of what I had made while I felt like my once promising career had been completely destroyed? Of course not, but only at the bottom you can see the light.

"In moments of darkness or confusion when others would flounder because things didn't go the way they expected or wanted, you can thrive if you shift your focus immediately to the new situation. Stop trying to deal with the old scenario or problem – it's gone. You have a new situation to focus on. If you can make that shift, and adjust to the new set of circumstances, address it swiftly, and holistically, and respectfully for all parties, you can make the best of the new conditions. Hopefully, you will have the foresight to protect yourself against potential downside as best you can.

"If you want what you think is real responsibility or glory or success in the selling game or upper management, you have to be able to handle what comes with it. But you also must keep things in perspective – you cannot carry the whole company or situation on your back alone. That was the other thing I had to realize. I thought ABM couldn't survive without me, and for sure my old division tanked when I was gone. But they did move on. They sold off – multiple times. A lot of those folks are still there, now with really high-level titles at a lower echelon company. But things move on. These decisions aren't life or death. If I can't close this deal, life continues. There's just a different playing field I face. And I try to face every one of them with fresh eyes."

"Inspiring, my friend," I commented. "I don't know a lot of people who have that perspective of the fast and furious flurry of an impossible sales situation."

"What choice did I have? My frustration – if aired publicly – only instills doubt in others. I handled each situation as I needed to. I immediately put the CEO e-mail on Dave Anthony's radar and explained the situation. I ensured the right contract was out to the CEO at the hospital, so our part was done. I had done all I could, and I had to be content with that fact regardless of results. That's the real trick. That's the balance. That's leadership.

"You think coaches go out wanting to have losing seasons? Of course not. The standings are even across the board, they formulate a strategy and a team, and they go forth. There's a foundation and variables, and then other things enter the equation – contests, egos, injuries, media, gossip and unplanned scenarios. All of the pressure falls on them. They carry the weight of the team whether other individuals are stressed or not. And you 'leave it all on the field.' That's what I had done here. Maybe they'd sign, maybe they wouldn't, but I had done all I could do."

"Did they?" I couldn't wait. I was always a guy who tried my best not to read spoilers, but sometimes I couldn't help it.

"It was Thursday when the CIO was back. He called me that morning and was asking about a credit he claimed he was expecting to see on the contract based on a conversation we had had over a month prior. It was a legitimate credit *seven* contract revisions ago, prior to them asking for more product and me managing to get them qualified for a better price level to get them to the dollar figure they claimed they had to get to squeeze this by the board.

"I explained that credit had been manually absorbed; I took it into consideration when I had taken this back to the VP to get a blessing on the new configuration and I fortunately found an e-mail from weeks prior where I had explained this. He claimed he felt like he had been misled. We were at a standstill.

"There was obviously nothing more I could do. I had to tell him, 'I understand this process has been taxing on us all. This is not only a fair deal, but it's far better than I ever envisioned we'd be able to put together for you. We took every single element that you claimed was important into consideration. We delivered the product, the services, the number. I'm hoping you can get it signed as you reflected you could,' and I left it at that."

"Wow. What did he say?"

"That he was going to try, but that based on these changes and the lack of credits he was expecting that I was making him look bad. He'd have to explain this to his boss. I get it – everybody needs a win, and nobody wants to look bad to their boss. You have to remember that when you're making a deal.

"This guy has a reputation he cares about and reports to someone at the highest level in their organization. I never thought there was any malice intended, and do believe he told his CEO that they were getting these certain line item credits. Not having them on the final iteration of the contract put him in a bit of a bind and meant he'd have to do some selling.

"That's why I always try to minimize the amount of my job I ask someone else to do. I even offered to talk to the CEO. But I didn't get there in this case. All I could do was wait and see.

"I had an open IM chat thread with Heath Nichols, the vendor rep who was managing the contract. Every so often Thursday and bleeding into Friday, I'd ping him to see if he had any update. Nothing. I messaged the CIO – Stan – to summarize the package, copying everyone on the team including Dave Anthony, just to reiterate the state of the union. As luck would have it, our contracts team was working the weekend as it was the last of the fiscal year so if I got a Friday signature the deal would get done. I just hate to cut it so darn close.

"It started early Friday. Most of it was through e-mail, but we were on the phone a couple of times, too – Stan and me. I think they expected me to flinch on this $121K credit they claimed they were expecting. They kept making it about that. I'm guessing Stan had presented it as that credit was on top of the numbers we showed them at $5.999 million. He said this additional expense meant they might need to take it the board.

"And you never know in those cases – is he saying it to get me to budge because he knows I want the deal, or is it trivial at this point?

"I couldn't budge. That was the deal – period. But if his degree of heartburn over that amount of money was really going to cost me this deal, I had to do something.

"I could *taste* the deal. I knew that landing this deal would catapult me from another good 100%+ year to 180% of my goal because it would maximize my accelerators in multiple payout buckets. I was going to do everything in my power to get this deal done and until it was signed, I would stop at nothing.

"I was up against everything in that moment. Those moments. Up against not only my failure with Quintana, but ABM, Cellular Horizons, Tel-Cell. My failures with Abby before we were married. I had the ability to be redeemed in my mind; I had been counted out by so many people in this organization as a has-been who was out of his element due to the Peter Principle and this one deal could change all that.

"They wanted $121,000? I was going to find it somewhere."

I shook my head. This guy. Unbelievable drive, motivation, and an unwillingness to back down until the deal's done. Not only that, but the fact he had enough mastery of the deal and the variables and the wherewithal to go back to some well – *any* well – for something else, showed what a student and master of the craft he truly was.

Never quit. Never say die.

"I had a different vendor on standby to do work with the hospital to build and customize the solution, provide training and help with the deployment," Vincent continued. "We had a little bit of funding already allotted to the project should it proceed. My first call was to the project leader to see what we might be able to do to either shave money off of their statement of work or apply for more funding. He was on vacation.

"My next call was to his partner, who had been part of each session and call we had had with the client while we plotted out what the customization could look like and sold this concept across the hospital business groups. He was out of the country, on vacation."

At this point, I am in disbelief. But he was not finished.

"I scoured every e-mail that this vendor had ever sent pertinent to this hospital project and found two additional names that had been included on *one* of the dozens of previous e-mails before. I had no phone number, so I sent e-mail requests. I went to LinkedIn and looked for folks in senior leadership at this vendor, sending connection requests in hopes I could get someone on the phone. I scheduled a call and invited as many people I could find to it based on those two addresses I could find and guesses at other addresses based on their listed name on social media and the domain name the two I found had.

"I had the call. One person showed up. I tasked him with finding *anybody* actually available at their organization who could help find *any* discounts they could apply to the statement of work. We went point by point of the SOW and looked for creative ways we could apply for more funding. I came up with about $100,000 I was willing to ask for should the hospital move forward.

"They were in touch with me throughout the day and found another roughly $50K we could shave off their SOW. All told, I found the equivalent of $154K in additional money we could either apply or subtract from the current expenditures they had on the table while keeping the deal intact.

"I took this back to Stan, crafted a comprehensive summary *again* via e-mail encompassing the deal for all eyes to see including their CEO, including everything we had invested with workshops and discovery leading up to the deal structure, the numerous revisions and value adds, and this $154K to address their concern over $121K.

"And then it turned out the CFO was off that day, so Stan wasn't sure he could get it reviewed."

"*What?*" I shrieked.

"Then Stan told me a bit later he would be back in touch with me by 4 PM with an update, 5 PM being the drop-dead cutoff to get a deal submitted.

"4 PM came and went. Nothing. 4:10, 4:20, 4:30 – nothing. At 4:36, I prayed to God.

"And I didn't pray for the deal, because I don't think God cares about sales. I prayed for my full circle redemption. I needed this – to feel like I had completely come back. From all of it. From ABM to Quintana. I prayed to feel completely whole.

"And at 4:37 PM CST on Friday, June 28, 2019, Heath Nichols IM'd me saying, 'I got it, bro!' Then Stan followed up with an e-mail. The deal was signed. Mission accomplished."

"Yes!" I exclaimed, hammering my hand down on his bar. "That is incredible! What a feeling!"

"It was. It was unreal. I couldn't believe it had come in. I couldn't believe the onslaught of calls that came in after that, congratulating me – led by Dave Anthony. It felt like *Rocky* or that moment at the end of *For Love of the Game* or any great sports film ever made. I was the champion."

There was a moment of silence between us, where I could tell Vincent was remembering basking in that moment and I was in awe of what he had just described. It had taken over 9 years since ABM had annihilated him and he had just kept crawling back, overcoming obstacles, winning in court, advancing little by little back up the ranks in his career and he had once again reached the summit of a mountain. His storied career had truly lived twice.

He could have lost the deal and had a really good year. A good comeback story by nearly every measurement. But - no – he had put an exclamation point on it with a mega-deal while all odds were against him.

"Best financial year of my life, too, but that was almost a byproduct. Knowing I had done it – against all odds and perception – and getting that recognition in that moment and in subsequent messages and calls was what validated me. I needed it more than I ever would have admitted."

He paused again, before adding, "And then, the scoreboard goes back to zero and all eyes are on you again to do even more."

I nodded. He was right. The seller's requirement to deliver more was never done.

"But I was going to do it differently this time," Vincent continued. "I knew I had to take a break. I had truly pulled out all the stops and given it everything I had, and I had to unplug. I was off from that day for the following 10 and came back for a few days before going to Jamaica with my family. And I *really* unplugged this time;

not like when I had no service due to being in the mountains, but by shutting off *all* of my notifications.

"We went to the Milwaukee area where my cousin's farm is on the Quincy side and stayed there a few days. Playing games, looking through old pictures, drinking beer. We drove to Millington, Tennessee, for a day to see Abby's brother Jamie Winters re-up with the Navy and drove back. Had some stellar Memphis barbecue.

"Abby and I would do stuff together and we'd split off with the girls and we'd just try to squeeze in as much as we could. I got to spend a ton of time with Sydney, too... she is such a ham. I love that kid so much. We'd eat Cheerios and watch *Star Wars* and go for walks and play Barbies and play outside.

"Some days we went out. Some days we were lazy as can be and stayed in and had food delivered. I just tried to shut my brain down. In the past, I had taken time off and come back refreshed and ready to take on the new week or month or – in this case – fiscal year. But I didn't want to.

"Abby was singing at church. Elizabeth was out of school for the summer and we played basketball outside and went to the park and grilled and had family over. Our vicar and his family came over for a game night. Stuff like that. What I envision normal people do all the time.

"The few days I was back at work, I had been asked to train an entirely different division on how I prospect. I got caught up on e-mail. That Friday, they made the announcement that our job no longer existed. The inside sales team would completely own the account relationships. I was going to become a technical data specialist for a larger territory if I stayed on. And I was announced as the President's Club winner for the entire field division the same day. It was bittersweet. And the following morning, we flew to Jamaica for a week."

"Very timely," I remarked. I shook my head. "So, you fight and scratch and claw for the winningest of winning seasons and they eliminate your job."

"Precisely," he replied. "Others had not been as successful in the role, so they got rid of the role entirely."

Whatever I could have said in that moment really would not have been all that perfunctory, so I remained silent and just shook my head again, swilling the last of the wonderful elixir.

Abby called down to us from upstairs that dinner was ready.

We ascended the steps, joining his girls around the dinner table. We prayed. The meal was delicious. They did a ceremony Vincent stated he picked up from a college friend's social media post years ago where they go around the table soliciting everyone's "Rose" (something great that happened to them that day), "Thorn" (a less-than-stellar occurrence or circumstance in the day), and "Bud" (something they looked forward to). I participated in the spirit of the occasion.

Vincent had jettisoned any outward sign of his feelings toward the events he had just shared. What had been a hard-fought, grueling fight to the finish to get a massive career win was quickly met with another defeat in his illustrious career. This had been a year ago. I knew at least this morning he was still at the CTMI building for some reason. But there was an ominous, unspoken theme here as he had met with them earlier, presumably to arrive at a new resolve of some sort in his career – either moving on or moving forward.

Whatever the news, he did not share it at the table. I can only assume he told Abby privately at some point throughout the day. But I would not learn the verdict until a bit later.

Vincent's wife, kids and I bid each other farewell as Vincent and I prepared to go. He was taking me to the airport for my flight home to St. Louis.

We got into his Aston Martin again. The air was cooler and a bit dry. He left the top up this time, given the colder temperature, checked mirrors and we were on our way.

"So - new gig, new year. What happened?" I asked, knowing our time together was drawing to a close soon. Certainly, we could continue the dialogue, but I definitely wanted to understand my friend's plight while I was in his presence.

"That same Friday before Jamaica, Jake Zuniga's role was completely dropped as well, and he wasn't offered anything. The guy had been instrumental in getting me to stay up until this point. We had worked together for over 3 years and had turned the market around completely. Now he was gone.

"I had never taken a trip before where I completely abandoned my exercise and diet, but Jamaica was that trip. I was in the ocean or pool daily with my family, eating whatever I wanted and keeping the refreshments flowing. I fell in love with my water shoes. The views, including even the one on our balcony, were breathtaking.

172

"We saw James Bond and *Cocktail* filming locations. I even had some naps! I needed a hard reset on my brain, my body, my soul. I'd get under the waterfall and just let it pour down on me. I fully expected it to shock my system back to a state where I could go back and do this new role and support Avery's business along with that of other reps I'd cover. I'd have another new boss - Doug Vance. And I'd have to get technical certifications – something I had no interest in doing.

"But when I came back, I had nothing left. Jake always warned me I'd burn out and I didn't believe it. But I had. I was toast. I didn't care, I didn't want to do this job. I was going through the motions.

"I took solace in that I was OK, my family was OK, and that I wasn't compelled to do anything – I could skate. Studies say 83% of workers 'mail it in.' I just never had. But now I felt like I was – with nowhere to go. I felt bad about it, but whatever I tried to tell myself, I could not get my heart or head back in the game.

"I was limping to 2020."

Vincent took the ramp for MN-62 E. The sun was setting, and the sky was a perfect blend of orange and purple and pink.

"After being out of pocket for basically July, I had to go to Dallas for kickoff at the start of August. I was in 'day at a time' mode. My personal brand was exceptionally strong.

"But at that point, I had to immerse myself in the role. I had no choice. We had 'territory planning' so we were bound to be diving deep into the new territories, new initiatives, etc.

"Fortunately, night one in Dallas is typically reserved for drinks, *Cocktail* and karaoke with Jeff Mason. That time did not disappoint. We had Whataburger and he made Red Eyes.

"The rest of the trip left quite a bit to be desired. It was a joint session between the inside sales and field sales organizations, and they tried to pitch a unified front. But what I got out of it was they did a lot of rah-rah baloney along with trying to train us how to do the jobs of our partner managers they had just let go. It was stupid motivational nonsense from a bunch of managers who were relatively brand new to the company or role, who probably wouldn't be around in a year or two anyway, spouting off platitudes and training us on the role they just dumped.

"What was billed as territory planning amounted to spending 40 discombobulated minutes with each rep and a few other team members on *Day 4*. Most of the additional team members weren't even in town. It was mostly 'I'll introduce you' to people you don't already know in the account. And then we flew home. Complete waste of time.

"I get it – I'm jaded. I've been doing this a long time. Heck, I was the guy getting up on stage selling dreams in crappy call centers. Now, these guys were doing it, and I could see through every silly analogy, every ridiculously unrelated sports parallel and motivational speech. I was actually put off by the whole thing.

"At least I got to see some old friends on the trip, like Jeff Mason, like my old buddy Jacob Wertz who was the one who told me to always 'follow the zeroes,' like Mitch Finkleson who I hadn't seen in a couple of years, like Fred Hampton – who had gotten hired on as one of my peers a few months' back. I always enjoyed seeing the old familiar faces.

"I just had to make it a few more months – I had earned President's Club and I wanted that trip to the Bahamas. I would make it to 2020 and then it would be game on. I had gotten 7 different opportunities presented to me in 2019; surely, I could garner some interesting offers for the new year. I'd start planting the seed right away.

"We got our quotas in early August and I had a 62% year-over-year growth required for the territory."

"Oh my – there's a smack in the face," I remarked. "I mean, 10%, 15% - those are customary. But *62%*?"

Vincent could only shake his head.

"I know. I'd psych myself into a day, only to be demoralized, unmotivated or dealt a setback of that magnitude every day before noon.

"So, I threw myself into stuff I enjoyed doing, like prospecting. Like blogging. I wrote a lot of company blogs and was featured on their webpage, which was kind of nice. I actually developed quite a following on there because of my already strong social media presence. By the end of the year, I was the #1 blogger on the site for social engagement company-wide."

"That's very impressive!" I stated.

174

"I figured if I was not in a role I wanted to be in, I'd incorporate what I enjoy into my role," Vincent offered. "I kept doing the stuff I enjoyed, like partner and technical specialist webinars, but I expanded them. With my social platform what it was, I could promote them to and with the help of colleagues and globally via social media. Thanks to that sharing, I'd get ten times the leads I was getting before just for myself, and many more for the partner in other geographies.

"But I was sleepwalking."

It had to be difficult to be Vincent Scott. A supernova who always just wanted to shine brightly in a world where nothing else was like him.

"The job itself just kind of existed. I had a ton of pipeline, because I had all of the old relationships. I just needed people to do more data projects. The first quarter, I exceeded goal without really lifting a finger. The first quarter quota was a bit of a layup anyway – it wouldn't be until third and fourth quarter when it would become unattainable.

"The primary new requirement was that I would have to get much more technical, studying for and passing a handful of certifications. They had handed the job I did well to people like Avery and now I was supposed to be a technical resource, driving 1 primary KPI as opposed to several. A lot less influence across the channel and with clients than I wanted or was used to. But, I had a job still.

"The President's Club trip – overall – was nice. It was much needed to leave for a week, even though we missed our kids. Abby's mother watched them all week, which gave us some pause because we had never been away from Sydney for even a day. But once we got there, we could bask in the warmer weather, the beach, the pools, the restaurants, even the unlimited drinks and snacks and room service – it came easily to allow ourselves to be pampered.

"The food was incredible. We went horseback riding. The views and the beach were out-of-this-world.

"But there was no award ceremony, like the old Top Gun trips at ABM. I won that award 6 times and every time they made me feel like a hero – calling me up on stage, speaking about the impact I made. This was nothing of the sort.

"And when it was announced that week that CTMI was building a whole team of internal sellers to specifically sell customizations on top of our platform, and they would need new leaders and a director to manage them all for the field, I sought out VP Todd Branson and GM John Lewis to express my interest for what I felt like I was the obvious choice. Todd never replied. John took my call...and he could not have seemed less interested.

"He had only been with our company for six months, and he handed the job to a buddy of his at his last employer's - a competitor of ours.

"That was when I realized it was time to go."

We were nearing the exit for MN-5 W toward MSP Airport. It was sunset, and it was beautiful.

I could have asked him why he felt like the only move was to go, but I knew. Not only had he come back from his ABM termination to finally surpass where he had been, but he had overcome another setback that would have finished or chased off most others in the same situation. He had proven he could do the job – better than anyone else – despite Quintana's best efforts to destroy him. He had done all this only to see his job eliminated, his cohort's job eliminated, and a promotion that should be his wound up going to a hiring manager's buddy. He had nothing more to prove in this role.

"I'm a loyal guy, but if ABM taught me anything it was to not blindly count on people to be loyal to me."

"So, you're leaving, huh? That's what that was about today?"

Vincent smiled. We were pulling up near the airport and headed toward Terminal 1.

"I started what I like to call 'passively looking' after getting back from the Bahamas," Vincent said. "It was the end of the calendar year, so I didn't figure much would shake out. But it did.

"The second folks started hearing that I might be interested in a conversation, floodgates opened. There were a few internal opportunities – one as a Director in the inside sales division if I moved to Dallas. Another as a services specialist working in Large Business Group. Yet another as a territory manager in our healthcare division.

"Accord Business Group was always interested in my candidacy. Another local partner also wanted me to come on board and run sales – even though they only had two sellers. And two previous co-workers wanted me to come work for them – one at a partner, and one at our largest competitor."

"Look at you! Quite in demand," I commented. "What did you do?"

We were pulling up near the departure gates. He parked the Aston Martin near Gate 4 and turned to me. His cellular phone was in the small tray below the dashboard, and he retrieved it.

After he input his passcode and accessed a document, he showed me the screen. And I knew.

"Very nice," I commented. "Congratulations."

I was practically speechless. Not only had Vincent come full circle over these last 10 years, but he was smiling. He was free.

"Thank you. And thank you for all of this. I trust you'll throw in a few witty things and pretend I said them," he remarked.

"I can probably handle that," I replied. "Thank you for a heck of a day. Heck of a story. It's always a pleasure."

I exited the vehicle, came around back and grabbed my bags. We shook hands. I looked at Vincent Scott – who knows when the next time I'll see him will be? Hopefully sooner rather than later, but even if it's in another 10 years I hope he's doing something he loves, impacting and inspiring others.

"Would you still consider yourself to be a 'salesman on fire?'"

Vincent considered this for a moment. He smiled. "We're all 'on fire' - with faith, with family, or friends, our work, our passion, our hobbies...sports, competition. Sometimes the fire has to be stoked or fanned – but it's there. As long as our light exists."

I liked that answer.

Epilogue

A few months passed, and I was putting the finishing touches on this story. The world had changed, though. We found ourselves in the midst of the coronavirus pandemic of 2020.

My life had changed pretty dramatically, shifting to remote work with the whole family at home, schooling virtual, parks closed and a stay-at-home statewide order.

Vincent Scott and I were scheduled to connect on a virtual call. We had messaged each other a few times since we got together nearer the beginning of 2020 in Minneapolis. I knew there had been some changes in his life as well, and I was looking forward to hearing about them. I was also curious his thoughts on the role of sales during the pandemic.

His face greeted me on the video call. He had a very full beard! His hair was not as short. He looked a little tired, but his personality did not show it.

"Vincent!" I greeted him as he came on. "How are you, my friend?"

"I'm good, Carson," he replied. "Busy. Adjusting to this new world. How are you?"

We briefly described our current state of the union along with apologizing for barking dogs and sounds of children in the background.

"So - sum up your life right now," I requested.

"It's interesting," he replied after a brief pause. "It's changed dramatically just over the last few weeks. But I'm glad I made the move I did."

"I bet," I replied. "And I'm curious, as there is a lot of messaging right now about how sellers should approach these times – what say you?"

"Good question," he answered. "Now, more than ever, the seller's job is about relationships. We can't connect in person, so it makes it all the more important to find ways to connect.

"Much of what we have trained or been trained to do is obsolete. Now, we have to reach out, check up on people, listen and try to find ways to help.

"Deals that are in flight might be at a standstill and priorities are all out of whack. Your customers are shifting to remote work. They are hoping to differentiate their portfolio in a way that keeps or shifts their relevance. Some companies are fighting for their survival.

"For some, it's a time of hibernation. Some sellers are getting laid off. It's the situation we are in – there is no control over the circumstances whatsoever. Our only choice is to persevere.

"Check on people. Check on family, friends, customers, colleagues, former co-workers. Everyone's world has been rattled. It's like God took the snow globe and gave it a good shake. The routines, the places we frequent, sports, meetings – they are all canceled until further notice. Now it's about staying mentally and physically fit, working from home, home-schooling and hoping you can find toilet paper."

We chuckled.

He continued, "A seller's job has changed in many ways, but has remained the same at its core – we listen. We are available. We are a resource.

"For those of us who are adept at pivoting and evolving and who have endured much in our career, it's still been a major change but the ability to slow down to focus on priorities and effectively use any gaps in our schedule will serve us well. It's a time to connect, but also to train. To read. To journal. I've journaled every day I've been in isolation.

"For a seller – for a leader – this is a time when more than ever your network relationships, personal brand and responsiveness matter. It's a time for non-sales outreach, checking on everyone you can, expressing concern, being available and making personal connections. Even though we can't see them face to face, we can absolutely send a note or engage in a video chat.

"It's a time to be a resource. Share insights that are helpful. Help your team, too – help colleagues and see where you can support your leaders. Be empathetic. Everybody has a vantage point right now. Some people are infected, but *everyone* is *affected*. I've looked for places to donate, I've supported local restaurants with take-out or delivery, and tried to help folks in my network who have been laid off."

"You referenced deals that are in flight right now. These are obviously forecasted pipeline for organizations who are banking on revenue for 2020. How do you keep these projects moving?"

"Respectfully," Vincent responded after a brief pause to collect his thoughts. "Obviously, these deals and relationships are sensitive. We've got to delicately communicate, but gently reiterate established priorities our customers indicated to us. We should have agreed upon timelines, milestones and action items. A gentle nudge toward some of these, to ensure we are honoring priorities they expressed, is not out of bounds.

"I will say, I've crafted some of the most passive 'sales' messaging of my life during this time. If and when I am talking to some of the major players within my client organizations, the conversations are shorter and I'm giving them every chance they may need to back out or change the agenda or cut it short - because it's all about them. More than ever before.

"You want to leave them with the impression that you're the seller who cared when their world got turned upside down.

"Outline what proceeding as you had planned might look like. Offer up some alternative ways to shift gears in light of circumstances. Ask for a conversation and listen to how their organization is adjusting.

"There was a direction you agreed you'd go in together, but it has undoubtedly changed.

"Something else that works is attempting to repurpose discussions that were in flight to suit new needs. Your customers are shifting to remote work, which has all kinds of collaboration, security, morale and continuity implications. If we change parameters of our talks, what different approach or input from your organization might assist them in being successful in any of their new priorities?

"Possibly more than ever before, and certainly in all new ways, your customers need ways to communicate, to collaborate, to endure – and to reach their client base. They are going through new challenges outside of work as well – home-schooling children while working full-time. Caring for or concerned for loved ones who are at risk. Some people are afraid. Challenge yourself and your suite of solutions – or maybe just your network and ability – to be timely and relevant in this environment.

"And then poise folks for what's to come. The best way for any company to position itself for rebound or a rebirth is to be strong in downturn and prepared coming out of it, meaning they need a strategy any time their cheese is moved. How can you help them and be part of that specific strategy?

180

"What will their organization's needs look like on the other side of this? What is of the most value to them internally and externally? How can you improve their data, their presence, their profitability – now and in the future?

"The distinct possibility also exists that you can't do anything right now. That was a real conclusion I came to during this time with some of the folks I worked with. But I still performed outreach, sent a newsletter, conducted informational events – I just tilted them to timely topics that I thought may resonate or provide a service.

"The best thing you can do as a seller or leader in uncertain times is stay consistent. You're still their advocate. You're still their responsive, trusted adviser. You're like Superman – you're just there. You're around.

"If you're an effective, available, respectful and resourceful leader for colleagues and customers alike, you'll emerge stronger.

"We're in a perspective-shaping and molding experience. It's full of opportunities to make you better as a professional and a human."

"Insightful, per usual," I remarked. "Thank you for that. How have you spent the time?"

"I've followed the rules. My team's clients pulled the plug on all in-person sessions pretty quick, and with Abby pregnant and at home anyway, and us taking turns home-schooling Elizabeth, I started working from home straightaway," he replied.

"Wait - Abby is pregnant?" I marveled.

"Daughter #3 due Labor Day," he remarked.

"Congratulations! That's fantastic! Man, you'll *really* be outnumbered!"

"Thank you," he replied. "We're excited. The kids are excited. The family is excited. And, yes, I'm destined to be a Girl Dad. That's OK. I love it. And even the pets are girls. We had a hamster once who was a boy – he did not make it."

We laughed.

"I've been reaching out to as many folks as I can. My best friends. Jack Johnson is in the Middle East with the Navy and can't go anywhere. Eddie Haskins is a teacher and had the last semester of school scrapped. We actually got on our first video chat the other day – I don't know why we didn't think of it until now. My brother-in-law Jamie is in New York with the Navy.

"My family. I was glad my Dad – who works part-time delivering for Cooke's Grocery Store back home in Mankato – got a reprieve and is at home.

"We went from very hectic lives running Elizabeth to and from basketball and volleyball practices, games and tournaments, constant work commitments and lots of activity to being homebound. Very surreal. We're also more connected than other with church because we can attend more church group stuff now that it's virtual. That has been nice.

"Abby had coached some of Elizabeth's volleyball, was singing in church and running her to volleyball practices, while I was out in meetings all day and on basketball practice duty and Sydney duty when Abby and Liz were gone. Now – all of that is obsolete.

"A bright spot is I've talked to my Grandma more during this time than I probably had in the previous year! She's told me stories I never knew."

"Tell me one," I requested.

"My Grandpa and Grandma had a farm. It's where my Mom and her three brothers grew up. She told me one story about how one of my uncles got out one day and went wandering around – and they found him near the creek! He could have died. Both my Grandpa and Grandma were tending to different things and had no idea. I never knew about that.

"My favorite was one day my Grandma came home from working all day. 17 people were sitting outside drinking and my Grandpa comes up slyly and says, 'we're all just waiting on supper.' So, she said, 'Great idea!', grabbed a beer and joined them. Told them if they wanted something to eat, they'd have to provide it themselves. I always loved her bluntness.

"She talked to me about her travels and how her favorite trip she ever took was a cruise to Alaska. I never would have known about these things had we not had these chats.

"Down time doesn't have to bring you down. Find productive ways to use your newfound margin. Ideally, it's a time to get closer to family and to keep connections that matter alive. Sometimes to even take them to a new level. Everyone needs to connect right now – more than ever.

"I exercise, read, write, do interviews, work, home-school Elizabeth and spend a ton of time doing things with family."

"How do you lead a team right now?"

"With care," he replied, without hesitation. "Handle with care. All of the familiar and faithful philosophies apply – the sales food chain dictates we nurture the relationships we can touch. We must understand the perspective of the people we touch – our leaders and our team members. And our colleagues.

"Invest time in finding out how they feel. Don't tell others *how* they should feel, just hear them out and try to offer what they think they are needing. Do they need time? Do they need advice? It's unknown terrain for a lot of people, so mostly *everyone* needs understanding and latitude. Listen and ask, 'How can I help?'

"This is a time when the ability to lead and work through ambiguity matters a great deal. There are not answers to a lot of the common questions on your team's mind. They are likely first and foremost worried about their loved ones. They want to know how their job or pay will be affected. They want to know how quota may be affected. And they are also working through massive changes on their home front on top of all of that. Listen, empathize, encourage.

"We don't know all the answers. Now, more than ever, there's no easy fix or response. But we are all human. We are all in this boat together. And we all have valid, genuine concerns.

"Project confidence and tackle one thing at a time.

"A lot of the importance I placed on other things certainly lost their luster during this time. I valued more than ever the fact that my family was safe, no matter what the threat. That I felt secure in my job. That no matter what happened, there was a path forward.

"And there was a ton of grace. Senior people I talk to are holding their kids or have noise and distractions in the background. I cringed when the dog barked on a conference call before. Now, we're kindred spirits when that stuff happens."

We both chuckled a little at that.

"Leadership is still about people and process. Just because they are thrown into upheaval doesn't mean we don't hone in on how we can best be at the pulse of one and best pivot to the other."

"How was leaving your previous role?" I inquired.

"It's amazing how you can look back at a time when there was a flurry of activity and tough decisions and know you did the right thing," he answered. "I spent much of the time since last July grappling with the 62% quota hike. I took on an expanded territory that had already been exposed to the inside sales team and some of them were so fed up with how they had been treated by that team they wouldn't even talk to me. They were actually canceling our service – so I was already behind the 8-ball.

"For me, it was in my mind I'd find something new for 2020. Jake Zuniga and I were still talking regularly, and he wanted me to join him – wherever that wound up. Nick Aragon was still trying to get me to reconsider Accord Business Group. Prens Koruyucu had left a few months' back to go to a competitor, and had already been promoted – and wanted me to come work for him.

"There were internal roles as well. As I told you when I dropped you off at the airport that day, I had the choice to take promotions into a few different divisions of Majestech-Ware or CTMI.

"The whole process was bittersweet; I still enjoyed working with what was left of my team – Johnny Smythe, Will Matthews, Fred Hampton and a handful of others. But I was shocked when Dave Anthony left shortly thereafter for the same partner Jeremy Rivers had gone to."

"Dave Anthony *left*? I thought he was on the fast track?"

"Crazy, huh?" he replied. "I was now working for Doug Vance – and I really liked him. Great guy. Religious, knowledgeable, loved motivational stuff. I felt like we were cut from similar cloth. He really enjoyed having me on the team. He seemed quite confident in my ability to succeed in the role. He tried to lobby for me to his boss, GM John Lewis, to be able to do more for the division. It all sounded great. But my heart wasn't in it. And it was time to go.

"I was forthcoming with Doug – that I was being courted internally and externally and was weighing a move, but that I wouldn't do anything without him being the first to know. I wanted to do it right. And I wasn't in any way concerned with being targeted for keeping my options open – not anymore.

"Then, it really heated up between a few of the potential offers. I'm a firm believer you have the conversations – all of them. Entertain them, see where they go, so you know what's real and what comes to fruition. Thing was, a handful of them became very real. And I was once again weighing decisions like moving my family, moving companies, changing roles completely.

184

"All the while, I was still being asked to stretch a great deal in my current role. Demands on my social media contributions and blogging were at an all-time high. Our President Kelly Jergenson wanted me to film a campaign for her on social selling.

"And then the funny, kind of ironic things started happening as well. Cooke's Grocery Store – who had unceremoniously dumped CTMI on me while I worked for Quintana – came back. They signed with us – which was quite unbelievable given the turn of events years before.

"Our VP Todd Branson made his first visit to Minneapolis – and I lined up a dozen clients just like I always did for Dave Anthony – and he was blown away. But he also pulled me aside and tried to convince me to stay in my role – selling me on potential growth and all of the things we could do together.

"It all sounded great, but I leveled with him about my struggles with the direction of the organization and my desire to have a greater impact.

"GM John Lewis called me one day, too, giving me the same pitch. And I told him the same thing.

"There was definitely a part of me that wanted to stay. But I knew I had to make a decision and go."

"How much of your current role can you discuss?"

"I can't discuss it today, but give me time," he said. His wink was evident through the video chat.

"So, we'll do this again?" I asked, with a hint of glee in my voice.

"I've learned to never say never."

AUTHOR BIOGRAPHY

Carson Vincent Heady was born in Cape Girardeau, MO, graduated from Southeast Missouri State University and moved to St. Louis in 2001. He has served in sales and leadership across Microsoft, AT&T, Verizon and T-Mobile.

Carson is best-selling author of the *Birth of a Salesman* series, the first book of which was published by World Audience Inc. in 2010. He released *The Salesman Against the World* in 2014, *A Salesman Forever* in 2016 and *Salesman on Fire* in 2020. He is also featured in Scott Ingram's *B2B Sales Mentors: 20 Stories from 20 Top 1% Sales Professionals.*

Carson is a 7-time CEO/President's Club winner across 5 roles at AT&T and Microsoft and National Verizon Rockstar winner. He has been recognized as a top social seller at Microsoft and is consistently ranked in the top 25 sales gurus in the world on Rise Global. He is included among the Top 50 sales authors on LinkedIn.

With over 330K social followers, Carson has also been interviewed on over 30 sales and leadership podcasts, by such luminaries as Jeffrey & Jennifer Gitomer, Jeb Blount, Brandon Bornancin, Sam Dunning, Larry Levine, Darrell Amy, Scott Ingram, Thierry van Herwijnen, Jim Brown, Sam Jacobs, Luigi Prestinenzi, Donald Kelly, Marylou Tyler, George Leith, Pat Helmer, Eric Nelson, Ron Tunick, Jeff Arthur, Mary Ann Samedi, Jean Oursler, Andre Harrell, Marlene Chism, Bill Crespo, Matt Tanguay, Josh Wheeler and Chad Bostick. He has also co-hosted the *Smart Biz Show* on EG Marketing Radio.

His articles have appeared in several noteworthy publications such as SalesGravy, Smash! Sales, Salesopedia and the Baylor Sports Department S3 Report.

Carson lives in St. Louis, MO, with his wife Amy and daughters Madison and Sidonia.